D1058595

Praise for
Action Learning

"As company president, I am concerned about the quality and quantity of our leaders. David Dotlich and James Noel write about real-life experiences, frustrations, and successes in addressing both challenges."

—Peter Jacobi, president, Levi Strauss and Company

"Global companies today must manage complexity and interdependency. This book provides ideas and tools for helping leaders succeed in demanding times."

—William Weldon, company group chairman,
Johnson & Johnson

"Action Learning is an effective and vital way to provide executives with a platform upon which to develop leadership skills. David Dotlich has worked with us for the past five years to strengthen the leadership and organizational capabilities Johnson & Johnson needs to win in the global marketplace. Through Action Learning, we are institutionalizing Johnson & Johnson's standards of leadership."

—Allen C. Anderson, vice president of education
and development, Johnson & Johnson

"Action Learning works. This book shows why."

—Marshall Gerber, partner in charge of partner development,
Arthur Andersen

ACTION

LEARNING

David L. Dotlich
James L. Noel

ACTION
LEARNING

How the World's Top Companies Are Re-Creating Their Leaders and Themselves

DAVID L. DOTLICH

JAMES L. NOEL

Jossey-Bass Publishers
San Francisco

Substantial discounts on bulk quantities of Jossey-Bass books are available to corporations, professional associations, and other organizations. For details and discount information, contact the special sales department at Jossey-Bass Inc., Publishers (415) 433–1740; Fax (800) 605–2665.

For sales outside the United States, please contact your local Simon & Schuster International Office.

www.josseybass.com

Manufactured in the United States of America on Lyons Falls Turin Book. This paper is acid-free and 100 percent totally chlorine-free.

Library of Congress Cataloging-in-Publication Data

Dotlich, David Landerth.
   Action learning : how the world's top companies are re-creating their leaders and themselves / David L. Dotlich and James L. Noel. — 1st ed.
     p. cm. — (The Jossey-Bass business & management series)
     Includes index.
    ISBN 0–7879–0349–3 (cloth : acid-free paper)
   1. Executives, Training of.   2. Executive learning.   3. Organizational change—Study and teaching.   4. Leadership.   I. Noel, James L., date. II. Title.   III. Series.
HD30.4 .D67 1998
658.4'07124—ddc21

                                   98–8887

HB Printing   10 9 8 7 6 5 4 3 2 1   FIRST EDITION

The Jossey-Bass
Business & Management Series

Contents

Preface   xi

Acknowledgments   xv

The Authors   xix

Introduction   1

Part One: Action + Learning = Change

1. The Action Learning Framework   13
2. Stories of Action Learning in Action: Three Types of Action Learning   35
3. Why Change? Rising to the Challenges of the New Business World   49

Part Two: Putting Action Learning to Work

4. You Can't Buy Leadership: Transforming Leaders in Place   69
5. Growing Global Leaders   83
6. Breaking the Boundaries Between Functions and Business Units   99
7. Reconceptualizing the Business   115

8. Releasing Fresh Thinking and Independent
    Action   135
9. For Companies to Learn to Change, People
    Must Learn to Change   149
10. Fusing Technology and the Business   161
11. Removing the Barriers Between Customer
    and Company   171
12. Reaching to the Future   185

Resources

 A. Recommended Readings   195
 B. Action Learning Examples   197

Index   205

Preface

This book is for organizations who realize that they need to find new
and better ways to develop their leaders. We have worked with
some of the best companies in the world—Citibank, G.E., Johnson
& Johnson—who have come to this difficult realization. They have
grasped that their various training and executive development programs are ill-equipped for the demands of a changing organization,
industry, and world.

As one CEO said to us: "Show me a leader who is decisive,
fiercely independent, dominant, and in control, and I'll show
you someone who doesn't have a clue about how to lead today's
organizations."

Unfortunately, many emerging leaders have been raised in cultures that prized traits such as unilateral decision making and rugged
individualism. Not only their cultures but their mentors and role
models have given them a false sense of leadership. George Patton
may have been a great general in World War II, but in today's military he would be a nightmare.

This book is for any manager who recognizes that it is no longer
enough to create leaders, we need to "re-create" them. Over the
years, we have helped companies all over the world re-create their
leaders through a process called Action Learning. We have done so
to help achieve the following objectives: To help key people learn
how to work and lead cross-functionally, globally, technologically,

and scores of other new and different ways. By using this process, we have enabled managers to identify their outmoded and negative traits and replace them with forward-looking attitudes and behaviors. We have given thousands of Action Learning graduates the ability to lead confidently and effectively in complex, paradoxical, and ambiguous environments.

In the following pages, you will find examples of how we have accomplished this and discover the process that makes transforming people who transform organizations possible.

We start out with a step-by-step description of the Action Learning process, followed by three mini-case histories of the process in action. Next, we present an argument for "re-creation" and against the traditional tools for developing leaders. The meat of the book consists of seven chapters that address the specific leadership issues that all organizations face sooner or later—issues that range from technology and the global marketplace to dealing with change. Each chapter demonstrates how companies can prepare managers to handle these issues effectively by using Action Learning. These chapters also include various tools that will help you analyze where your company stands on these issues and how Action Learning might benefit the company in these specific areas. We conclude with a discussion of how these issues will evolve in the coming years, and suggest certain trends that will make leadership re-creation an even more compelling concept.

Some of the issues that we discuss in this book have been around for a while. Developing leaders who can function effectively in the midst of rapid change, for instance, has been the subject of many articles, speeches, and books. What is new, however, is the growing frustration with programs that fail to meet this and other leadership challenges. We have heard CEO after CEO bemoan the difficulty of helping their emerging leaders learn to manage in a team-based environment or shift their focus from functional to big-picture thinking.

In response to this growing level of frustration, we offer this book. We have seen first-hand what Action Learning can help people accomplish. We have orchestrated Action Learning programs whose impact on individuals and organizations has been nothing less than metamorphic. People can change, and they can change quickly, dramatically, and in ways that dovetail with larger organizational goals.

When companies first started using Action Learning, they often viewed it as their secret leadership weapon. We honored their desire to keep it a secret. Over the years, however, the word has spread. Too many well-known organizations have incorporated Action Learning into their development programs for it to remain a secret.

Just as important, the need for Action Learning in organizations all over the world is growing. Executives are struggling with leadership issues like never before. The confusion and debate over how to confront these issues are tremendous. So many changes are occurring so fast that getting leaders up to speed and able to handle unfamiliar, evolving roles sometimes seems impossible.

The task, however, is not impossible. Action Learning is a process that can develop new leaders effectively, now and into the next century. After reading this book, we believe that you will possess the knowledge and tools necessary to re-create dynamic leadership.

Acknowledgments

Many clients and colleagues have contributed to and supported Action Learning. At Johnson & Johnson—Allen Anderson, Gerry Kells, Inaki Bastarrika, Barbara Lagouri, Marta Liano, Carine Degreve, Mike Fruge, Diane Sedden, Efram Dlugacz, Bill Weldon, and Roger Fine were consistently helpful; Val Markos and Melanie Cadenhead are beginning the adventure at BellSouth; Noel Tichy has been a friend and colleague for fifteen years, and his inspiration is found throughout this book. At Levi's—Pete Jacobi, David Schmidt, Linda Reid, Bob Haas, Gord Shank, and Donna Goya have contributed their insights; my Burke colleagues are the best teaching team ever—Steve Rhinesmith, Peter Cairo, Neville Osrin, Neil Johnston, Mark Kiefhaber, and Claude Lineberry. Nationsbank colleagues also inspired this book: Jim Shanley, John Harris, Rob Ball, and Chuck Cooley. Jerry Meyer at Tektronix has always supported me, and Judy Oppenheim and Bill Miller at Avid Technology are eager to try new things. Phil Carroll and Linda Pierce at Shell Oil hung in there when the chips were very much down. Also, many clients and colleagues in various companies over the past years have supported Action Learning: Deborah Barber, Terry O'Connor, Pat Case, Karin Kolejdski, Karen Mailliard, David Walker, Ken Smith, Marshall Gerber, Deb Himsell, Patti Stacey, and Dorothy McGlauchlin. Arnie Kanarick has been a mentor and friend since the beginning. Tom Pinkson and Mary Knecht have shown me how to complete the circle. Cedric Crocker at Jossey-Bass saw the potential of a book on Action Learning and nurtured it. Finally, three people deserve special mention: Amy Beacom for managing both me and the editing process; Steve Knecht, who is always there; and Doug Elwood, who inspires everything.

Portland   David Dotlich
January 1998

The insights and experience gained over a career are shaped by many people. Unfortunately, space limitations do not permit a complete accounting. A number of individuals, however, have had special impacts: Ram Charan with his penetrating questions, energy, and integrity; Noel Tichy, a truly creative visionary; and Edgar Boone, who early in my career, opened doors to possibilities I had previously not considered.

Colleagues with whom I have worked most closely and want to thank include Daisy Brownstein, Pat Matthews, Steve Mercer, Betty Disch, Doreen Collins, Vi Janssen, Martina Keane, and Anne Leavy. Finally, those who offered assistance and direction include George Bair, Bob Holland, Gene Andrews, Jim Baughman, Paul Van Orden, Tim Sullivan, Jim Dagnon, Victor Menezes, and Larry Phillips.

New York   Jim Noel
January 1998

To Doug, Carter, and Jeremy
—David

To Sarah, my wife and best friend
and our children—Allison, Amy, and Ted
—Jim

The Authors

David Dotlich has been involved with planned organizational change in academics, business, government, and consulting for twenty years. He has served on the faculty of the Michigan and Minnesota Business Schools and is a consultant to the top management of Johnson & Johnson, Levi Strauss & Co., NationsBank, Bell South, Sprint, Nike, The Limited, Merck, Arthur Andersen, Citibank, and other companies in organizational change, executive coaching, and executive development strategies. He is a certified psychologist in the areas of career development, life planning, and numerous psychological inventories. In addition to co-authoring this book on Action Learning with Jim Noel, he is co-author with Peter Cairo of *Action Coaching*, to be published by Jossey-Bass in December 1998.

From 1986 to 1992, Dr. Dotlich was an executive vice president of Groupe Bull, a $7 billion computer manufacturer headquartered in Paris with 45,000 employees worldwide. He was responsible for all internal and external communications, including the award-winning advertising campaign, "Know Bull," and for human resource and quality improvement activities throughout the world—with emphasis on leadership training, compensation, and recruitment programs needed to reduce cycle time, control costs, and shift a large hardware manufacturer quickly into new businesses such as services, software, and consulting.

Until 1986, he was vice president of human resource planning and development for Honeywell. Responsible for worldwide training, selection, affirmative action, and research, he spearheaded the formation of Honeywell's Management Development Strategy, Corporate Conference and Training Center, and also led corporate-wide projects such as One Honeywell to present a unified product offering to diverse customers from various divisions, and the Honeywell Job and Relations study, which surveyed 5,700 managers worldwide and identified how effective leaders develop and create winning environments for people.

Before joining Honeywell, he was on the faculty of the University of Minnesota, where he taught in the business school and in the Department of Speech-Communication. His teaching and research focused on the impact of the organizational culture in producing effective leaders, with special emphasis on women and minorities. His consulting company designed change programs for clients such as IBM, the Federal Reserve Bank, 3M, and the Farm Credit System.

His interest in people development began with a first position as a social worker in the Cincinnati inner city. After receiving a B.A. degree from the University of Illinois, he obtained a fellowship to study in Race Relations at the University of Witwatersrand in Johannesburg, South Africa. While there, he conducted survey research on racial attitudes in the African townships. After returning to the United States, he joined the U.S. Department of Commerce as a training director assigned to Minneapolis and completed an M.A. at the University of Minnesota, where he also received his Ph.D.

David Dotlich has taught for many years in the executive development programs at Pennsylvania State University and the Universities of Michigan and Minnesota. At Minnesota he designed the highly successful "Leading Human Resources in the 1990s" executive program. At Michigan, with Noel Tichy he led the Change Leadership Consortium, which brought together line managers from six Fortune 500 companies to develop as change agents in their respective organizations. He is on the boards of directors of Schmidt Industries and Ash Creek Ventures Fund.

Jim Noel has a consulting practice specializing in organizational change and executive development. His perspectives on action learning and organizational transformation were heavily influenced by his tenure as manager of executive education and leadership effectiveness at Crotonville, General Electric's famed Management Development Institute. Most recently as vice president of executive development, Jim initiated Team Challenge, Citibank's organizational change process, and an executive development program utilizing an Action Learning format. Other positions in industry have included vice president of staffing and development with the Burlington Northern and Santa Fe Railroad and director of executive development for Philip Morris.

Jim started his career as an academic as assistant dean, College of General Studies, at George Washington University in Washington, D.C. He lives with his wife Sarah in New York City.

ACTION LEARNING

Introduction

When we began using Action Learning in the mid–1980s, we were both struck by its unique ability to address issues of executive development and business strategy. At the time, we were at companies—Honeywell and General Electric—that needed to address both issues simultaneously. Honeywell and G.E. were attempting to make enormous changes. To make them effectively, they needed fresh strategic initiatives and people with the vision and capabilities to carry them out. To transform their companies, they had to transform the emerging leadership's attitudes and behaviors—or, as we have termed it, they needed to *re-create* their leaders.

We did not invent Action Learning to achieve this goal. The term and the concept had been around in various forms for years, though it was sufficiently esoteric that not many people outside the executive development field knew about it. On its most basic level, Action Learning is nothing more than learning by doing in a controlled environment. People like University of Michigan professor Noel Tichy and consultant Ram Charan helped elevate it far beyond this basic level, and we would be remiss if we did not mention their contributions right from the start.

Over the years, however, we have run Action Learning workshops throughout the world. We evolved and fine-tuned the process for a variety of world-class organizations: Ameritech, Citibank, Johnson & Johnson, Arthur Andersen, Shell Oil, NationsBank, BellSouth, Nortel

(Northern Telecom), and Levi Strauss & Co., among others. Because of our experience, we understand the unparalleled power of Action Learning to confront the issues bedeviling organizations today. Company after company has used it to map highly effective new business directions and to develop the executives who can lead organizations in these directions.

This book draws on our experiences. Perhaps the best way to introduce you to them is to recount each of our first encounters with Action Learning to capture how it almost magically met the ambitious objectives of our organizations.

David

When I joined Honeywell as corporate vice president of development in 1981, I became part of a company that was part of an industry that was about to undergo massive changes. For many years, Honeywell had been fat and happy, a mainframe computer manufacturer that enjoyed great profit margins and captive customers. Its culture featured swashbuckling salespeople who made huge commissions and regarded service technicians as a lower corporate life form. Given the margins and captive customers, complacency was widespread. Honeywell also maintained the fierce independence and isolation characteristic of others in the mainframe computer industry.

Some people in management recognized that this golden era was about to end. They saw the coming of the personal computer. They realized that they would no longer have captive customers and would have to fight fiercely for a share against traditional competitors and untraditional ones—and that the competition would eventually become global.

How could we prepare Honeywell's key people to compete in this radically new environment? How could we encourage in-bred Honeywell managers to consider other, foreign viewpoints? How might we help them question the status quo and prompt an emotional acceptance of change? What might catalyze them to communicate their fears about the future and reflect upon their role in it?

As someone fresh from academia (I had been a business school professor at the University of Minnesota) and the world of consulting, I was well aware of the possible answers to these questions. We could fly in the world's leading experts to talk to Honeywell managers about change; we could hold encounter groups that would allow them to deal with the emotional issues; we could send them off to other companies to benchmark changes there or to executive development programs where they could study case histories.

None of these options, however, was viable. The ego of Honeywell's best and brightest would make them defensive and unwilling to listen to the experts. Mainframe computer people did not believe anyone knew their business as well as they did; they considered themselves unique. They would also deem encounter groups as so much silliness, unrelated to the reality of their jobs.

Honeywell's president understood that he needed to put his people through an "experience"—something that would engage them intellectually and emotionally in the changes that would soon sweep through Honeywell and would cause them to reassess and possibly change their behaviors and attitudes.

I contacted Noel Tichy, a professor at the University of Michigan School of Business Administration. Together we set up what we privately referred to as "strategic boot camp," which later became known as Action Learning. The goal was to have participants wrestle with the same difficult strategic issues that so concerned Honeywell's president and search for what they could do as individuals and leaders to confront these issues. We rented a rural meeting center called Gainey Farm and brought 150 Honeywell executives there for three workshops spread out over a three-month period. During and in between workshops, these executives were energized and exhausted, frazzled and dazzled. They became interviewers and researchers, talking to experts who previewed the coming of the personal computer age. They worked as a team to scale walls and engage in other challenging outdoor activities. They put together predictions and recommendations about the company's future and what should be done, reporting directly to the president. They were given tools and opportunities to reflect on their own behaviors and determine how they might help or hurt the organization in the future.

The results were revelatory. One revelation was that these Honeywell executives could open themselves up to new ideas and approaches—ideas and approaches that they would have shunned before the workshops. By the end of the process, a number of them were challenging cultural assumptions and lobbying for change. At one point, a team held a mock funeral in which they symbolically buried elements of Honeywell's past. Just as important, however, were the recommendations that emerged from Gainey Farm. The reflection, feedback, interviewing, and teamwork all contributed to the breakthrough thinking and solid proposals for reshaping Honeywell. These were not pie-in-the-sky recommendations; they were well thought-out and well researched. Ultimately, the recommendations helped Honeywell make the wise decision to return to its core competence as a control manufacturer and sell off other parts of the business.

Jim

Before arriving at General Electric in 1984, I too had spent most of my working life in academia. With an M.B.A. and a doctorate in adult education, I had been involved in university executive development programs and continuing education. I joined G.E. because of the opportunity to work at their Management Development Institute at Crotonville, a facility that was considered one of the leaders in executive education. I arrived in the early part of Jack Welch's revolution. He was transforming G.E. from top to bottom, attempting to flatten the structure, create a boundaryless organization, empower teams, and make many other dramatic changes.

Though Crotonville's general manager program was state of the art, it was not capable of re-creating G.E.'s leadership. Patterned on Harvard's program, it relied heavily on traditional case histories.

Although it offered participants great materials from great teachers, it did not significantly touch people's attitudes and behaviors, nor did it stimulate the visionary ideas and strategies that Welch was demanding.

When Welch brought Noel Tichy in to head Crotonville in 1985, Tichy brought the same Action Learning concept that he had helped David implement at Honeywell. Together with Tichy, consultant Ram Charan, and others, our group began turning G.E. into a learning laboratory for teams of cross-functional executives. We assigned big, strategic marketing projects to them and set them loose to find new ways to grow GE markets. In support of their efforts, we provided the coaching, team-building tools, and feedback participants required to develop as leaders of the new G.E.

Watching participants emerge from this Action Learning crucible, I recognized that what was taking place at Crotonville was as revolutionary as what was taking place within G.E. We had discovered a way to transform function-focused managers into cross-function ones, to change individualists into team players, to shift people's emphasis from their departments to the customer. It was clear to me that Action Learning would be an invaluable process not only for G.E. but for any organization facing major change issues.

As a Citibank vice president of executive development, I helped implement Action Learning as part of the Team Challenge program and saw it perform the same miracles that it did at G.E. Despite a completely different environment and objectives, Action Learning has helped Citibank transform its emerging leadership and implement a challenging business strategy.

A Versatile Process

When we met and began discussing our experiences on Action Learning projects, we shared a sense of excitement about the process. We were excited because we realized that Action Learning was not just another HR process with limited efficacy, it was a business process that would help companies build their next generation of leadership.

That organizations become aware of Action Learning and how it helps transform organizations and leadership is crucial. More than ever before, companies are struggling to transform their structures, cultures, and people. They are struggling, and frequently failing. Traditional executive development approaches that rely on case histories and other tools are products of an earlier era—an era in which the pace and magnitude of change was much slower and smaller than it is today.

This book on Action Learning is not simply an executive development book or even a book on leadership. Action Learning addresses the diverse issues spawned by change. The beauty of Action Learning is its adaptability; it can be and has been used to achieve a range of goals.

For instance, we will discuss how organizations activate the Action Learning mechanism when they are confronted with a major business dilemma. NationsBank turned to Action Learning when they were stumped about how to stimulate growth—they wanted to make the switch from relatively simple external growth (acquisitions) to a more complex internal strategy of innovation, new products, and other tactics. Ameritech relied on Action Learning when they were facing life after deregulation and needed to forge a new, more competitive strategy. Honeywell used Action Learning when they were attempting to deal with the rapidly approaching upheaval in the computer industry. These organizations recognized that the traditional responses to business dilemmas—hiring a strategic consulting firm, benchmarking, and problem-solving analysis—were not up to the challenge posed by their respective dilemmas. The issues were too complex and ambiguous, and they needed a process that could handle complexity and ambiguity.

In the following pages, you will find examples of organizations that turned to Action Learning to re-create their leaders in a number of different ways. Johnson & Johnson has relied on it to broaden the skills and vision of their top managers. Arthur Andersen has been running Action Learning workshops to transform their senior partners from auditors to trusted business advisors. Other organizations hope the process will help their top people adapt to new cultural and marketplace realities and give them the skills to help others adapt.

You will also find a third type of catalyst for Action Learning. We will talk about the organizations who have turned to Action Learning to deal with an immediate operational challenge. Many of Shell Oil's Action Learning projects, for instance, have the goal of growing revenue or cutting costs. Other operational challenges include integrating technology into work design and output, managing a virtual organization, managing talent on a global basis (rather than on a functional or unit basis), finding ways to engage employees (especially in the customer service area) through new communication technologies, and managing intellectual capital. Unlike the more general business dilemmas discussed above, these highly specific operational challenges must be met immediately. Action Learning accelerates the problem-solving process and helps participants view these challenges from multiple, synergistic perspectives.

As you read our Action Learning stories, you will find that some organizations are addressing all three issues simultaneously. Most often, they are attempting to re-create their leaders so they can better deal with business dilemmas and solve operational problems.

This Book Is Not for You If. . .

As enthusiastic as we are about Action Learning, it is only fair to issue a few words of warning. Although Action Learning is usually highly effective, sometimes it is not. It fails to live up to expectations when management

- Is not involved and supportive of the process

- Does not believe that Action Learning teams can make valuable recommendations

- Is not committed to a significant level of executive development and organizational change

Viewing Action Learning as a minor HR process rather than a major business intervention is a mistake. This attitude will communicate to participants that management does not take the process seriously. For it to be effective, participants need to know that management considers Action Learning critical for both participants and the company.

This is not a book for people who believe that leaders can be trained in classrooms, or that leaders naturally emerge and there is nothing anyone can do to facilitate or accelerate that process. This is not a book for people who are skeptical about an individual's capacity to change his or her behavior and attitudes.

We hope our readers, like our clients, subscribe to the belief that individual leaders can be re-created, and that by so doing, organizations can foster major strategic changes that otherwise would be difficult if not impossible to make.

Spreading the Word and the Model

We are constantly amazed at how many organizations still rely on traditional methods of executive development and change management. Despite overwhelming proof that most of these methods are ill-suited to the demands of the workplace in the late 1990s, they are still widely used. Perhaps the problem is the lack of an alternative—a problem we hope to remedy with this book.

The first chapter offers a model of the Action Learning process, a model for setting up what is really a temporary learning system. It will help you understand how to construct an environment that is rooted in the real business world but sufficiently separate to allow the taking of risks and exploring of new behaviors. The model is brought to life in a number of ways throughout the book, including

- *Storytelling.* We have collected numerous anecdotes and illustrations of Action Learning from a variety of organizations. These stories are from both the individual participants' and organizational perspectives, and they bring the model to life.

- *Issue focus.* We have structured many of the chapters to address the issues that concern our Action Learning clients. One chapter, for instance, concentrates on how the process can be used to deal with customer issues. Another chapter examines how Action Learning helps companies come to terms with changes wrought by technology. A third looks at the role of Action Learning in breaking down functional silos and building a holistic team mindset.

- *Actions and Learnings.* You will find a number of exercises, thought-provokers, and lists at the end of the issue-based chapters to help you apply the Action Learning model and concepts to your own organizations and personal development and leadership concerns. Though not a how-to book, this book does suggest some ways to test the Action Learning process and analyze how your company might use it.

More than anything else, we hope this book excites you with a different way of developing leaders and strategies. Many of you might have become frustrated in your attempts to launch change initiatives or develop new leaders. You may have decided that your culture was too deeply ingrained to change or that a given person's managerial habits were too tough to break.

Action Learning can change cultures and break habits. It engages the whole person, not just the cognitive or emotional aspect. If you are familiar with any personal behavioral change process— quitting smoking, dieting, exercising—you know how difficult it is to make change work over the long term. Just as some executive development programs inspire people to make changes in how they manage and lead when they are still fresh from the program, the effect is short-lived. Sooner rather than later, people slip back into old patterns.

To catalyze permanent changes requires a more integrative approach. Action Learning is holistic. Personal goals are linked to organizational goals. The process requires people to exercise their intellectual, emotional, and even spiritual muscles. People come to see the relationship between their career progress and organizational change. Action Learning takes places in an intense environment where participants must reflect upon their values, challenge their ideas, and take risks with their behaviors.

It is a process that makes a lasting impact on both the individual and the organization, and it is one we look forward to sharing with you.

Part One

Action + Learning = Change

1

The Action Learning Framework

In the beginning, no organization asked us for Action Learning or for the "re-creation" of their leaders. Companies had heard about our workshops and how they helped organizations and individuals grow and change. They were intrigued by a tool that seemed to help people deal with evolving realities. They wanted their most promising managers to acquire the skills to perform in a global marketplace, a reengineered organization, a new competitive environment, in team-based structures, and in a rapidly changing, technology-driven world.

Some of these companies were in a crisis mode. Their survival depended on helping their people to think, act, manage, and lead differently. If, for instance, the next generation of leadership could not adapt to the requirements of a global business, they might as well pack up and go home. Other companies looked into the future and foresaw major problems if they did not start developing their key people in new ways. They recognized that they could no longer afford the luxury of having managers who disdained cross-functionality, teams, and diversity. Their five-year business strategies demanded certain competencies and behaviors from pivotal managers, and if those managers did not develop, the strategies could not be implemented effectively.

It was not as though their organizations were incompetent in the area of executive development. General Electric, Ameritech, Shell,

NationsBank, Citibank, Arthur Andersen, and Johnson & Johnson all had excellent developmental programs. They simply had not encountered the type of challenges presented to them by shifting business paradigms. How were they going to be able to convince someone who had managed one way for ten years to metamorphose into someone else? People needed not only to change the way they managed, but to examine and reshape fundamental aspects of who they were as individuals.

Companies have tried everything to help their people and their organizations make this shift, but the results were disappointing. Certainly, some executives emerged from executive development programs with new ideas and perspectives, but in most cases, the lessons learned did not last. People slipped backed into old managerial habits, and little was accomplished. Companies were frustrated because their strategic goals were on target but their emerging leaders were not capable of achieving them.

When organizations heard about what we had accomplished through Action Learning, they were intrigued. What magic could be involved?

Action Learning is magical, at least in the sense that it kills two birds with one stone. The process helps organizations respond to major business problems and opportunities, and at the same time develops key people so that they have the capacity to lead organizations in the desired strategic direction.

When we describe this process for top executives, they always ask, "What does an Action Learning program look like?" We assume the same question is on your mind. Describing a typical Action Learning process is not always easy; its implementation can vary significantly from company to company, depending on specific objectives and time frames. Still, most organizations that use Action Learning employ most if not all of the following twelve-element framework:

1. Sponsor
2. Strategic mandate

3. Learning process

4. Selecting participants

5. Forming learning teams

6. Coaching

7. Orientation to the issue

8. Data gathering

9. Data analysis

10. Draft presentation

11. Presentation

12. Reflection (debriefing)

Before looking at each of these specific elements, we would like to give you a general sense of what an Action Learning experience is like.

The Gestalt

Although Action Learning programs can have different time frames and structures, they all involve an alternating series of workshops with field experiences. The workshops are designed to provide participants with insight, information, and tools. They may involve everything from guest speakers who provide information to thought leaders who shock and provoke; they often include coaches who help participants understand the issues involved in their projects and give them tools that facilitate their ability to complete the project successfully. Field experiences range from outdoor adventures that help teams grow and work together, to data gathering and team meetings.

Though innovative and unusual techniques are certainly a part of this process, what sets Action Learning apart is how learning is interwoven with action. Participants are asked to address real and challenging business issues, but they do so within a "temporary system" created by the Action Learning process. This system encourages participants to make discoveries about themselves as they try to solve business problems; it provides teammates and sometimes a coach to help with this self-discovery and places them in unfamiliar situations with types of people they have never worked with before. Although a great deal of pressure is placed on people to perform, there is also a great deal of freedom to experiment and try new ideas and approaches.

Perhaps the best way of describing Action Learning is as a parallel universe, one that bears similarities to a given company's work environment but that is also distinct. Accomplishments that might take months or even years to happen in the real business world occur in a matter of weeks. Learning and action are compressed in intensive workshops and field experiences. When teams meet to formulate recommendations that they will present to the company, the sessions are unlike any other team meeting people have attended: They are more intense, confrontational, and focused. Action Learning forces people not only to think out of the box, but to think about who they are—as managers, leaders, and individuals. This change enables the participants to re-examine their company in a new light. The juxtaposition of who they are and what they need to do is always highlighted.

Let us now examine the twelve elements that hold this parallel universe together.

Sponsor

Without the backing of a significant sponsor, Action Learning programs cannot succeed. Other training and executive development programs may move smoothly forward for years without this support. These programs often are very well established within organizations and industries and come with stated outcomes; they can be controlled, predicted, and charted. Action Learning is much less easily controlled or charted. It is difficult to measure whether participants have become more accepting of diversity or whether they will be more open and flexible as leaders. As a result, Action Learning is vulnerable to political maneuvering and criticism. The business recommendations that result from Action Learning are measurable, however.

Sponsors play a critical role throughout the Action Learning process; and the more clout they have, the smoother the process goes. Paul Van Orden, G.E.'s senior vice president of marketing, embraced Action Learning as a means to an end. He wanted to find a way to get an engineering-dominated company to pick their eyes off the drawing board, open their mouths, and talk to customers; and he recognized that Action Learning could help achieve this goal. CEO Jack Welch was focused on helping G.E. become a global company. He wanted key executives to learn how to survive and adapt to unfamiliar business cultures. Again, Action Learning fit his purposes. With the support of these sponsors, Action Learning became a critical and continuous part of G.E.'s business and executive development strategy.

At Citibank, Victor Menezes wanted to find a way to break down functional and business unit silos and get people to look at the business in its totality. Even though he had only occupied his position for one month, he was willing to take a risk and sponsor Action Learning; he saw the risk as worth taking because he believed Action Learning was a method that might achieve a highly ambitious objective.

Let us assume that you have become interested in Action Learning and want to use it to achieve goals within your organization. If you are the CEO or a business head, you are the perfect sponsor. But what if you are someone else and want to convince a top executive to become a sponsor? Here are some tools you can use:

- *Demonstrate how Action Learning scratches a strategic itch.* Action Learning is not just a development program, and it is difficult to sell to a sponsor if you only focus on that aspect. It also helps organizations achieve

key strategic objectives, and we have found it makes
sense to let a potential sponsor talk to sponsors at other
organizations to understand the strategic benefits.

- *Inoculate the sponsor against resistance.* Sponsors need to
know that sometimes people protest against Action
Learning. "We are too busy for this stuff" is a common
complaint. Sometimes participants whine after the first
session or two: "It is taking me away from my real job"
or "I don't get the point." You may also anticipate
political resistance—Action Learning is threatening to
people who are invested in the status quo. Preparing a
sponsor for these possibilities helps lessen the impact of
the resistance.

- *Stress its multiple applications.* Action Learning can be
tailored to meet multiple objectives. Some organizations have used it as a succession planning tool: The
people who perform well in an Action Learning crucible become front-runners for key positions, even suc-
ceeding the CEO. Others focus on developing leaders.
Still others find it to be the best possible way to motivate people to accept and promote change: Sponsors
can shape Action Learning to carry out their agendas.

As you will see in the coming chapters, Action Learning is not
for the faint of heart or for the undisciplined organization. Sponsors
need to understand that this is an emotionally charged, intellectually challenging process; it demands that participants confront their
own failings, the failings of others, and the failings of the organization. We have found that companies with strong management and
disciplined cultures get the most out of the process. They are strong
enough to address the issues raised in an organized, structured fashion. Organizations with unfocused management and an ill-defined
culture can have problems with Action Learning: They may feel

threatened by the results of a program; they may lack the decision-making structure to take action based on what was learned.

Sponsors need to address these issues. Specifically, they need to ask, Does our organization have the discipline to handle an Action Learning program?

Strategic Mandate

In most cases, a business imperative drives Action Learning. It begins when management determines that a major business issue is affecting or will affect the organization, and that the processes that are in place are insufficient to deal with it:

- At Citibank, the issue was the company's mentality, and top management saw Action Learning as a vehicle for looking at the business from a broader perspective.

- At Shell, the driving force was the company's inability to earn the cost of capital, and the need for people to confront this fact and their misperceptions of the company's financial strength.

- At Ameritech, deregulation was fast approaching and managers were ill-prepared to work effectively in a new, more competitive environment.

- At General Electric, the strategic mandate was to turn a company of domestic-minded engineers and managers into global thinkers.

- At Johnson & Johnson, a big issue was upgrading human resources around the world and developing executive talent.

As you can see, these are matters of consequence. We refer to them as *stretch* issues, in that they demand that people stretch their thinking and behaviors to deal with them. Action Learning programs are catalyzed by stretch concepts; they are designed specifically to transform people in ways that other training cannot.

Do you need people who have never been out of the country to feel comfortable working in a Third World country? Do you want buttoned-down, by-the-numbers executives to start thinking and acting creatively and more openly? Action Learning is designed to give people the chance to experiment with new ideas, behaviors, and beliefs. When you see a mismatch between a major business goal and managerial ability to carry it out, Action Learning is appropriate. It is where a business imperative intersects with an individual development agenda.

Strategic imperatives are translated into Action Learning projects. Participants, usually in teams, are briefed on an issue and asked to produce a recommendation that addresses a problem or an opportunity related to the imperative. Directly or indirectly, everything that takes place in an Action Learning program is designed to help participants come up with a viable recommendation.

Learning Process Roadmap

How is all this going to unfold? How will you do the team building? Where does coaching come in? How and when does the process address key business issues? These and other questions are frequently asked by potential sponsors, clients, and other executives. Because Action Learning is new and unfamiliar, sponsors are naturally concerned about the specific elements of the process. Consequently, we often provide them with a roadmap of sorts—a written chronology and description of how an Action Learning process is likely to play out.

Roadmaps vary. For example, some companies remove participants from their jobs, and all their time is consumed by the Action Learning program. Other organizations expect participants to carry on with their regular work while participating in a program. These two approaches result in very different time frames. Similarly, some companies have us assign individual work projects while others prefer team work projects—again, the roadmaps diverge. One Action Learning program may require participants to do a great deal of traveling between workshops (to gather data for a team project and meet with team members), whereas another program can be conducted in one specific place without much time between workshops.

With all these qualifications out of the way, let us look at a roadmap constructed for an Action Learning project, Citibank's "Team Challenge" (see Exhibit 1.1).

The chronology of the "Team Challenge" Action Learning program is diagrammed. Though specific events such as Talent Inventory Review, Team Building, and Project Debrief are common to many programs, the ingredients of the event may take different forms. Do not be concerned if you are not sure what takes place in each event listed—we will clarify that as we go along. The model presented in this chapter is really nothing more than a master roadmap from which specific roadmaps flow. The next section of the chapter, Selecting Participants, corresponds to the Talent Inventory Review listed in Citibank's model.

When we use these roadmaps, we always ask sponsors to view them as flexible tools. As the process moves forward, we sometimes find it useful to tweak the process a bit. There is no definitive roadmap form. Perhaps a sponsor merely needs a time line and a list of issues that will be addressed. Still, a roadmap is useful, especially for an organization's first Action Learning program.

Selecting Participants

One selection criterion is the strategic mandate and resulting work project. You obviously need to choose people who will have an impact on that mandate. For example, if the strategic issue is implementing

Exhibit 1.1. Citibank's Team Challenge: Roadmap of an Action Learning Process.

Selection of issues and participants

Issues recommended by business heads or CEO
- Real, significant, and impactful
- Cut across businesses and impact total Citibank performance

Participants
- Recommended by business units
- Based on "talent inventory review" process
- Done on a worldwide basis

Team building and orientation to issues (off-site, 3–4 days)

Purpose and objectives
Introduce coaches
Team building exercises
- Diverse (business, geography, and function) teams of 6–7 people
Overview of issues and deliverables
Background presentations
- Experts, best practice companies, existing data, and so on
Team planning time

Data gathering (2–3 weeks)

Travel both inside and outside Citibank
- Customers
- External best practice companies
- Internal best practices
- "Experts"
- Focus groups (internal and external)
- Senior Citibankers or those closest to the issue

Data analysis and development of recommendations (1 week)

Data analysis and development of recommendations (1 week)
Debrief data gathering
Formulate recommendations
Draft presentations
Coaching

Presentations

CEO and business heads
- 90 minutes per team (30-minute presentation, 60-minute discussion)

Debrief and reflection (1 day)

Structured debrief with coach
- Recommendations
- Team process
- Individual development opportunities
Individual learnings and action plans
Celebration

Senior management follow-up (within 1–2 weeks of presentations)

Decision on actions to be taken
Assignment of responsibility for implementation
Continuous update on project status

technology, some participants should either be familiar with or influenced by that topic. As a general rule, diversity is a goal: The mixture of people from different backgrounds, functions, business units, and levels of responsibility creates tensions that facilitate learning. Because Action Learning is designed to identify and develop an organization's emerging leaders, most often participants should represent the best and the brightest.

These guidelines, however, often fall victim to internal political realities. "We can't leave Roger out; he'd be offended" and "If you can pick Susan for the program, then I should be allowed to pick Mary" are just some of the comments we have heard as executives argue over who should be chosen. Action Learning will not work if cronyism and politics dominate the process. Neither Action Learning nor any other developmental program can re-create a mediocre employee who is ill-suited to a leadership role.

When sponsors have difficulty determining who should participate, we use the following two tools:

- *Post-it notes.* Put the names of all possible candidates on Post-it notes where everyone responsible for selection can see them. Then the selectors pick the people who they believe should participate, reject those who should not, and put a question mark next to those about whom they are uncertain. The idea is for each selector to discuss and challenge other selectors' choices and arrive at a consensus about who the company's future leaders really are.

- *The change question.* Sometimes when selectors are unsure about a candidate, we suggest they think about the following: If you were to ask five people in your company whether the candidate is a change agent, has breakthrough ideas, and makes an impact on the business, how would they respond?

It is not just the selection process that is important, but how participants react when they are selected. If they perceive the selection as nothing more than being forced to participate in another worthless training exercise, they may be already negatively predisposed to Action Learning. The rigors of the process require people to be excited and energized about participating. If they are not, they may resist and fail to involve themselves.

Sponsors, CEOs, and other key executives must communicate that the experience can enhance both the organization and an individual's development. At Citibank, Victor Menezes gave each participant one of his favorite books and included a personal note about how pleased he was that they were engaged in this effort to help change the company. At Shell Oil, participants were personally invited to participate by Shell Oil CEO Phil Carroll.

Forming Learning Teams

Although some Action Learning programs, such as at Arthur Andersen, involve individual work projects, most involve teams. The team dynamic is the crucible where confrontation, conflict, new perspectives, and great ideas emerge.

Though participants certainly have worked on teams before, they probably have never worked on teams with both task and learning as goals. Unlike most teams, Action Learning groups contain people from different backgrounds, functions, business units, and hierarchical levels. In many instances, team members are chosen based on their differences and potential for conflict rather than their similarities and synergies. At Shell Oil, for instance, we debated whether to place a very powerful, hard-driving woman executive on a team with a manager who had sexist leanings. At first we were reluctant to do so: "They will kill each other," was one reason voiced against pairing them on the same team. The argument for doing so, however, was that if they did not kill each other, they would learn a lot in the process. We decided to try them out together, and though there was conflict, they both learned to deal with each other and to work together productively. We created their learning context.

In another Action Learning program, we deliberately included at least one business head from a foreign country on teams (most members were Americans). One of these teams was struggling mightily with a thorny issues, spending days in intense debate and discussion. During one particularly frustrating session, an American yelled at his Japanese teammate, "We've been talking and trying to figure this out for days, and you just sit there. You never say anything!" To which the Japanese executive replied, "All you do is talk; you never listen." The subtleties of cultural assumptions and values, often unconscious, had begun to emerge.

There is no formula for picking members of teams, other than the overarching goal of getting a good mix of functions and perspectives. One of the issues that always comes up is whether to include "subject experts" on Action Learning teams. If, for instance, the team is going to focus on global marketing issues, should you include a participant with global marketing expertise?

At General Electric, we always excluded these experts from teams. The reasoning was that these experts would dominate discussions and decisions, preventing the free-for-all debate that creates emotional and intellectual sparks. These experts would naturally attempt to deal with issues the way they dealt with them on the job, discouraging other team members from taking new approaches or stifling the "naive view." Still, many organizations include one or two subject experts on Action Learning teams, ensuring that someone can bring a certain amount of expertise and experience to the subject at hand. To avoid having these people dominate team discussions, teams are coached in team-building skills and understand that the process does not benefit when full participation is lacking.

Coaching

Not just any coach will do. For coaching to work in an Action Learning context, the coach must understand the social architecture of groups. Understanding that architecture is crucial, because the coach will be intervening in team situations where emotions run high and individuals are vulnerable. It is not a job for the inexperienced or the faint of heart, nor is it a job for an employee of the organization—someone who has to worry about politics, stepping on people's toes, and other organizational agendas. Ideally, a coach is an outsider with insider experience, someone who is comfortable working in interdisciplinary groups and who combines great intuition with superior communication skills.

Coaching is a distinct role and a distinct process—Action Coaching would be a more appropriate description. The goal is to accelerate learning. In a typical Action Learning program, the coach meets with individuals and teams at various points. Coaches often orchestrate team-building outdoor activities (rafting a river, climbing a mountain) and frame-breaking projects (working at a soup kitchen in the inner city) that occur at the beginning of the program. They also provide feedback and encourage reflection about various actions the team takes, from gathering data to making a presentation to the CEO.

Action coaches intervene directly in behaviors, confronting, challenging, questioning, and complimenting. "How are you going to get this presentation done in under ten minutes?" he might ask, or, "What might you do differently to avoid having everyone on the team upset with you?" The coach's interventions are not limited to questions. They often use 360-degree feedback to better understand the development needs of participants. Feedback is connected to something participants do in connection with the Action Learning project. They may have been insensitive to other team members' concerns or may have failed to incorporate another function's perspective in recommending a tactic. The coach's ability continuously and consistently to intervene as people struggle with real-world issues can have a transformational effect. More than anything else, the coach gives participants issues to think about and work on. The coach catalyzes reflection after every action. The alternating currents of action and reflection power the transformational process.

Orientation to Issue

Every Action Learning program has a traditional educational component—typically bringing in professors, thought leaders, and other experts to share new information with Action Learning participants. This information can run the gamut. We have had people come in and talk about why an organization might go out of business unless they make significant changes; we have had others discuss what really adds value to a business; still other experts have examined best-in-class issues.

The point is not simply to add to the participants' store of knowledge. Each stimulus provider is chosen based on his or her ability to help participants reframe the issue at hand. They are talking about something that directly relates to a given Action Learning project, and participants are challenged, provoked, and even shocked by what the speakers have to say.

Action Learning re-creates leaders in a variety of ways. Working on cross-functional and cross-business teams, rafting a river, receiving 360 degree feedback, making a presentation to the CEO, reflection—all these elements work together to reshape individuals in relation to the business and their jobs. The transforming power of information, however, should not be overlooked. Though it is more passive than the other activities we have mentioned, gaining information can nonetheless knock people out of their ruts and force them to reframe their orientation to the issue.

Data Gathering

Data gathering refers to a different type of information than that discussed above. As Action Learning participants grapple with a business issue, they are required to seek out relevant information from various unique sources. That means interviewing customers, vendors, analysts, benchmark companies, employees, academics, and industry leaders. It is not as though Action Learning participants have never looked at a market research report, but many of them have never gone out in the field and talked intensively and directly to so many different information sources.

This data gathering process has an impact on each participant's perspective. There is a big difference between reading a report and going out in the field, talking to a customer, and discovering new ideas and facts yourself. It creates a visceral, gut-level understanding.

This is not always a comfortable exercise for leaders. At times they are literally or figuratively in foreign territory, asking difficult questions and hearing answers that surprise or shake them. Their discomfort, however, is again part of the Action Learning methodology—people simply will not consider a different perspective if they are perfectly comfortable. As Peter Drucker has said, it is what we know for sure that most imperils us.

Data Analysis

Although the data analysis aspect of Action Learning sounds dry and dull, it is nothing of the kind. When people return from the field and meet with their teams, they are energized by what they have learned and anxious to share their knowledge and apply it to their work project. What occurs next is significantly different from what takes place in a typical team meeting for the following reasons:

- *The team is unlike any team they have ever been on before.*
  The unusual mix of functions and other heterogeneous

factors create natural sources of conflict and differing perspectives. Discussions are often heated, intellectually rigorous, and confrontational. There is also a competitive element to the teams that make people want to excel and win.

- *Stretch issues challenge both the team and individual members.* Action Learning teams are dealing with difficult, thorny problems; they are grappling with issues that are perplexing, confusing, and frustrating. For example, "What business should we be in? What is our future?" As a result, tensions run high as teams push themselves to understand new data and act upon what they find.

- *Pressure to perform is intense.* At the conclusion of Action Learning is a presentation to a top executive, a presentation that can have a profound impact on business direction. This awareness drives the team to perform, pushing them to sift through the data quickly, intelligently, and innovatively, while debating the benefits of taking risks versus playing it safe.

We have seen intense late-night sessions in which team members slug it out over what constitutes important data and what this information really means. Individuals search hard and long to prioritize the data and frame the business issue within the context of the data.

Given the volatility of teams analyzing data, we frequently provide them tools to deal with mountains of information. Early in the Action Learning program, we help the team practice using organizational skills—skills that enable them to break down massive blocks of data into component parts. Teams learn how to send individuals or pairs of people out for certain information, including how to benchmark other companies productively, and integrate their findings into a whole.

Draft Presentation

There is an obvious overlap between data analysis and putting the presentation together. The presentation is the performance element of Action Learning, and working on the draft is like being in rehearsal. This is the stage in which participants have to distinguish the real from the ideal. Typically, they are excited about the information and ideas they have gathered; their analysis may lead them to conclude that they have hit upon something significant. In their benchmarking, they may have seen a wonderful innovation at another organization and want to implement it in their own company.

Part of Action Learning involves forcing people to think systematically, politically, and realistically. Coaching interventions are often useful in this regard. For example, a political mapping tool can give participants a way to analyze the key players in an organization and where they stand on an issue. The goal is not just to create a good presentation; it is to create one that has a good chance of being successful. Anticipating, understanding, and managing internal political dynamics is a valuable lesson for participants.

Presentation

The final presentation is where the knowledge gained from weeks of Action Learning is put to the test. The goal is always to secure a commitment from the sponsor to act on the team's recommendation. If this is impossible, then the secondary goal is to prompt the sponsor to articulate what she needs in order to give that commitment.

Presentations are short and to the point. They are designed for teams to communicate their recommendations concisely and convincingly. After teams present their recommendations, the sponsor and other executives comment and question. Though presentations are not intended to be inquisitions, they can be stressful. Before making a commitment to act on the team's suggestions, sponsors put the team's ideas to a rigorous test. CEOs like Jack Welch at G.E. and John Reed at Citibank are not easy sells.

The atmosphere is electric at presentations. Many Action Learning participants have never made a formal presentation to the CEO or a business head. People who go through these presentations never forget the experience.

Part of the reason they do not forget is that their recommendations are often implemented. Action Learning is not just about learning new things and developing new competencies and perspectives, but about accomplishing deeds that have an impact on the business. Every Action Learning program positions the recommendations of participants as serious and significant. If the presentation is perceived by participants as merely an academic exercise, they are disappointed and disillusioned, and may become more resistant to future change efforts than if Action Learning was not attempted.

Presentations must include assignments to follow up on recommendations. The sponsor may assign an individual to gather more data and report back within a given period; he may assign someone to oversee a program of implementation. Whatever it is, accountability is paramount. Due dates are set, and people are assigned tasks. At Citibank, presentations end with a 30/60/90-day schedule— within each of these time frames, the team is asked to determine what they need to make their recommendations actionable.

Reflection (Debriefing)

Self-reflection is what distinguishes Action Learning from normal work. We often open each session of Action Learning with the question, "As you look back on what you did yesterday, what did you learn?" We also sometimes ask participants to keep a journal describing their feelings about what is happening.

At the conclusion, however, is a wonderful opportunity for people to think deeply about how the Action Learning process has influenced them. Participants have gone through an intense experience, and now that it is almost over, they are ready to contemplate it and discuss what they thought of it and how it affected them. We catalyze this reflection in a number of ways, including asking questions such as

- What would you have done more or less often as you look back?

- What do you wish you would have done to make it better?

- How would you have conducted yourself differently?

We have used a variety of tools to facilitate reflection. One simple technique is pairing team members so they can give each other one-on-one feedback. Another approach is to ask each participant to zero in on one behavioral change they would like to make as a result of their experience: What do they want to work on, and are they willing to make a commitment to change? This gives their reflection an action component that is often beneficial.

A third tool is asking each participant to write an observation about another team member on a Post-it note and putting it on the wall for everyone to read. The observations are along the lines of "describe what you think your team member should do more of, less of, or continue as is." A typical observation is "You insist on having your own way in team discussions; you are inflexible." When all these notes have been posted, each team member can pick one that applies to himself or herself and ask for examples of this behavior or just a general discussion of it.

At G.E., one Action Learning participant was younger than the others on his team, a brilliant top business school graduate who had done very well in his fast-track marketing position. During the final reflection session, team members told him that he probably had the best chance of anyone in the room of heading a major corporation some day, but that he would never achieve that goal if he did not learn how to work with people. Team members told him that as brilliant and analytical as he was, he needed to leave his "graduate school mentality" behind and recognize that winning every debate was not the only skill he needed. A year later, we ran into this participant again, after he had just received a major promotion. He told us that what he learned from Action Learning had helped his career more than any other feedback he had ever received.

This final phase is also designed to create closure. Teams usually are disbanded, and this is a chance for everyone to blow off steam and celebrate. Parties are common at the end of the program. Although reflecting and talking seriously about the experience is a great benefit, it is also important to provide people with an emotional release from all the tension they have been under.

Variations on a Theme

This twelve-element framework is sufficiently flexible that no Action Learning program looks exactly like another one. As you will see throughout this book, the tools that are used comprise one of the most common variations. For instance, there are all sorts of ways to teach people how to work together in teams. At Shell Oil, we gave teams the assignment of building rafts, putting their sponsor on the rafts, and taking him out to the middle of a lake and back without getting him wet.

We should also note that because Action Learning can create high tension levels, we look for different types of fun activities to break the tension. Having participants make a funny video can be a good tool for blowing off steam as well as building collegiality. We have also had teams work together in a gourmet restaurant, preparing a meal and serving it together. Other teams have played with and observed members of a symphony orchestra. These innovative team activities teach teamwork, interdependence, and mutual support.

We do not ask organizations to shape their objectives to fit Action Learning; we shape the program to meet their organizational needs. Action Learning is naturally pliable, accommodating a variety of conditions and concerns. In the next chapter, we give you a detailed look at two organizations and how Action Learning met their different business and developmental requirements.

2

Stories of Action Learning in Action
Three Types of Action Learning

Throughout this book, we refer to a variety of organizations that have used the Action Learning process. As valuable as these examples and anecdotes are, they only tell one small part of a much larger story. As much as we would like to share case histories of all the companies we have worked with, such an approach would result in an egregiously long book.

Still, it is important to "experience" a few Action Learning programs in detail. The process outlined in the previous chapter gives you a sense of what Action Learning is and how it evolves; this chapter is designed to give you an insider's view of the concerns and issues involved in specific programs. We translate the framework from the previous chapter into nuts-and-bolts activities and behind-the-scenes strategies, helping you understand the thinking of program participants and Action Learning sponsors.

Action Learning as a Mechanism for Cultural Change

Like many companies that embrace Action Learning, Citibank recognized the need for change and had a top executive who was committed to making change happen. The company had gone through a difficult period in the late 1980s and early 1990s. Though the situation was much improved when they began their first Action Learning program in 1996, Citibank was aware that significant issues remained to be addressed—issues that if left unresolved could inhibit Citibank from reaching its strategic objectives.

Victor Menezes had just been appointed chief financial officer, and he was acutely aware of the need for both organizational and individual developmental change. The need for change was rooted in Citibank's culture. Specifically, the culture embraced the notion of "letting 1000 flowers bloom." What this meant was "sprinkling" Citibank people all over the globe under the assumption that if they were empowered, they would develop and blossom. Such a philosophy had a number of benefits for Citibank, but it also produced a serious drawback: silos. The culture failed to link different offices and business units, thus allowing people to "do their own thing." Although this promoted an independent spirit, it also prevented the synergies crucial for a global company. Menezes found that many issues that cut across Citibank's five business units were not being addressed or were being addressed by different units in different ways.

Menezes wanted to find a mechanism that would allow people to view the bank in its totality. He wanted to break down the silos, and he wanted to deeply embed a new set of leadership skills in order to create managers with a revolutionary mindset.

Action Learning was a mechanism capable of achieving these goals. Thus began what Citibank called Team Challenge. With Menezes as the sponsor, Citibank moved forward with its first Action Learning program. The strategic mandate was to break down barriers that were inhibiting Citibank's growth and profitability. Citibank designed specific projects for teams that would help them fulfill that mandate. One project, for instance, called for a team to create a shared business service center. In the past, Citibank's five business divisions operated autonomously. There was little cross-selling; multiple statements were routinely sent to a customer of two or more Citibank businesses (a customer would receive one statement from the credit card unit, another from the branch banking unit, etc.); database information was not shared.

The first project challenged people to break down these barriers—not only the tangible barriers but also the intangible ones. Citibank wanted to melt deeply ingrained resistance to working cross-business and cross-functionally.

Team Challenge began with seven teams of seven members each. Participants were selected from a "high potential" group, taken off their jobs for one month, assigned to Team Challenge, and told they would be held accountable for their work by making a presentation to Citibank chairman John Reed and business unit heads.

All participants were aware that Team Challenge was going to be unlike anything they had gone through before. To take people off their jobs for a month was highly unusual, but to have them make a presentation to the chairman of the company was extraordinary. What participants did not know was that they were going to be challenged on many levels. The goal was not simply to come up with a new idea for a shared business service center; it was to work in new ways with people they had never worked with before to achieve the strategic mandate; it was to push themselves intellectually and emotionally and learn new ways to lead and manage.

Citibank's Team Challenge process was similar to the Action Learning framework discussed in Chapter 1. The "forming learning teams," for instance, began with teams going to Glen Cove on Long Island and working on team building. This included outdoor activities as well as discussions about how participants wanted to run the team, make decisions, and communicate within a team setting. Remember that many participants came into the project with a "silo" mentality; they were not accustomed to working on teams, especially teams of peers from different functions and business units. These team-building activities were critical, since dissension can easily tear an unprepared team apart in the heat generated by Action Learning.

"Orientation to the issue" and "data gathering" were the next steps. By bringing in outside experts and through discussion, Citibank helped teams come to terms with what "managing change" really means. These steps gave them an understanding of organizational structure through studying case histories and best practices. Teams were sent into the field for two and a half weeks to interview scores of customers, employees, and others about issues related to their project.

When team members reconvened and analyzed their data, the sessions were intense. Coaches intervened, stopping the action to determine what people were learning, why they were moving in a given direction, why the team was not moving as swiftly as it should. Participants, confronted with negative behaviors, became aware of individual strengths and weaknesses.

After teams made draft presentations to their coaches, they presented their findings to John Reed and business unit heads. Citibank has used about 80 percent of the recommendations contained in these presentations to move toward a shared services center and tear down other barriers between business units.

Action Learning as a Mechanism for Developing People Faster and Better

Citibank has run a number of Action Learning programs, but the following is quite different from the one described above and demonstrates the flexibility of the format.

Because of Citibank's "let 1000 flowers bloom" philosophy, it had not spent much time on developing people. It was assumed that they would develop themselves (and certainly some entrepreneurial types did). The problem was that the world—especially the financial world—had become much more complex. Few people bloomed on their own. Instead, they became locked into certain ways of doing things and certain ways of thinking—ways that were often functionally focused and change-averse.

Larry Phillips was Citibank's new senior HR executive, and he played the same sponsorship role as Menezes had. Phillips focused on developing the company's top three hundred people, the assumption being that the company could build business unit performance by building the capability of its key people. The first program concentrated on the general manager group—individuals responsible for P&L, developing business strategy, and integrating functions. Most of these people were Citibank country heads or in charge of a product line.

The Action Learning process for this project took place over a nine-month period and included alternating seminars, coaching, and on-the-job learning through Action Learning projects. Unlike Citibank's previous Action Learning program, this one put a great emphasis on participants' turning their jobs into learning laboratories. During the process, participants chose projects related to their jobs; they were asked to focus on something that would significantly enhance the performance of the organization. The idea was for them to apply the "learning" from the seminars and coaching to the "action" of their real jobs. The seminars and coaching facilitated work on the projects, providing skills and shaping behaviors that participants needed to complete their projects (see Exhibit 2.1).

The first seminar for participants was devoted to diagnostics, a common component of Action Learning. Citibank manages by a Balanced Business Scorecard, which includes people management, franchise growth, strategic cost management, community participation, and financial performance. For each element of the Balanced Business Scorecard, participants learned a set of diagnostic tools that they could use to analyze the effectiveness of their organization. Diagnosing the state of the business is a key skill; it was one that participants had to learn in order to move forward with the right type of project. Participants gathered in small groups and learned to analyze different facets of the organization. It was a self-discovery process facilitated by coaches. The feeling was that the more Citibank managers discovered on their own, the more enthusiastic they would be about acting on their discoveries.

After this session, participants were assigned a task: "Return to your job and identify one or two breakthrough changes that, if made,

Exhibit 2.1. Business Manager Leadership: Achieving Breakthrough Performance.

Learning Seminar I

Critical skills development
- Strategy
- Service quality and branding
- Strategic cost management
- Risk management
- Technology management
- People management

Balanced scorecard diagnostic assignment

People diagnostic

360-degree feedback

Form learning groups

Business Application I

Apply diagnostic tools
- Select 1–2 high-leverage areas of the balanced scorecard

Practice new people skills
- Interviewing skills

Apply people diagnostic
- Performance management
- Talent inventory
- Reward systems

Learning Seminar II

Review Business Application I
- Debrief balanced scorecard application
- Review people skills application and diagnostic

Provide team and change skills
- To implement balanced scorecard projects (Application II)

People management skills
- Feedback and coaching
- Talent inventory
- Development planning
- Reward systems

Business Application II

Assemble change teams
- Identify specific actions toward high-leverage areas of balanced scorecard
- Gain organizational commitment

Implement action plans

Apply new people skills

Learning Seminar III

Debrief
- Balanced scorecard projects outcomes
- People management
- Leadership, teamwork, management debrief

Personal development plan

Feedback to chairman/business leaders

would have a significant impact on the organization." By talking with their bosses about this change and receiving approval to make it, participants identified their Action Learning projects. To give you an idea of what types of projects people chose, here are a few excerpts from their written descriptions of what they wanted to work on:

- Franchise growth—develop a clearly articulated strategy that will address acquiring new clients and build our franchise.

- Put the right people in the right jobs—years of management changes and lack of attention to human resource management have created an environment in which numerous people are in the wrong jobs.

- Strategic cost management—find ways to release resources for future development. I will identify projects that will free up at least $5 million to be reallocated from back office to the front office to help grow the franchise.

At the second seminar, the focus was on the technology of change. Given the projects they had chosen for themselves, participants needed a "theory of the case." What makes change happen in organizations; what is the best way to manage it; how do you make sure it takes hold and lasts; how do you implement it? After three and a half days of intensive discussion, self-analysis, and coaching, Citibank managers left armed with a strategy for turning their Action Learning projects into reality.

After launching their Action Learning change projects, participants met a final time, five months later, for a debriefing session. Everything from issues of individual growth to strategic organization emerged during this last session.

Throughout the Action Learning program and especially at the end, participants tested and stretched their capacity for change (all projects had a significant change component); they also confronted ingrained behaviors that could potentially sabotage their projects. For instance, one manager kept insisting that he was never going to achieve his project goal. Through 360-degree feedback from his coach and intensive analysis of how change really happens at Citibank (and his role in either promoting or preventing it), he discovered elements of his management style that roadblocked change. Because his project was so important to him and because he had the opportunity to integrate learning with that project, this manager developed new leadership skills. He became more flexible, more willing and able to work cross-functionally, and more astute about his role in the change process. Of course, he may have learned these skills eventually, but instead of the learning taking years, it took place in a matter of months.

Raise Revenue or Cut Costs

Now let us switch companies and look at how Action Learning unfolded at Shell Oil. For Shell, Action Learning was a way to help its leaders define and execute a new business strategy. Whereas the company wanted to develop new leadership competencies, its primary goal was to improve the company's performance through Action Learning.

Like many organizations, Shell embraced Action Learning in response to a business challenge. Shell Oil had been hurt by low oil prices in the 1980s, and their overall return on investment was too low. Their inability to return adequately the cost of capital created "Shell-shock"; it catalyzed Shell's management to look for a way to reverse the company's fortunes. Shell's parent, Royal Dutch, was demanding higher performance, and a new CEO wanted to imbue a performance mentality in the company's best and brightest managers. By changing the culture, they hoped to facilitate implementation of a new, performance-oriented strategy.

Shell Oil's Action Learning program began with an off-site workshop for their executive committee, in which they defined a future state for the business and decided to mobilize their top managers. Working over a period of several months, the executive committee and sponsor CEO Phil Carroll decided to launch two series of Action Learning programs. The first series focused on strategic imperatives facing the business and included topics such as creating growth, integrating technology infrastructure, business planning, and capitalizing on the Shell Oil brand.

Shell's strategic series began with a workshop in which the business case for change was presented in graphic detail. The goal was to shake people up, challenge their assumptions, rouse them from their comfortable culture, and provoke them to action. An important aspect of the workshop was that many of the people attending it were engineers by training; they were linear-thinking and logical individuals. They did not change their minds or their attitudes easily. It was not enough to tell them that even though they were part of one of the world's richest and biggest corporations, their performance did not equal that of much smaller, more nimble companies. Mere telling does not have much impact on behavior and ideas.

The second series of Action Learning workshops focused on operational improvements of the business and required leaders to make an impact directly on the bottom line. These workshops helped Shell leaders realize the seriousness of the threat to Shell and that they had to change as leaders to stay in business. This workshop fostered this realization in a number of ways, including the following:

- *Presenting the business case.* Many of Shell's managers did not realize how serious the situation was; many of them had grown up in a company that was so big and dominant, it had to be successful. During this workshop, Phil Carroll, the CEO, and others talked with them about the financial numbers and shared some projected numbers with them; outside presenters, such as Professor Larry Selden of Columbia Business School, discussed what the best in-class performers were doing and how they were doing it.

- *Choosing a project that would raise revenue or reduce costs.* Between workshops, participants led a team on a project designed to achieve either of these objectives. This was the only criteria, and it drove home how serious management was about fostering a performance mindset. These projects were undertaken in addition to regular jobs.

- *Building team development skills.* Most leaders needed new ideas to mobilize teamwork around short-term operational issues. Coaches helped teams create a plan for working together and gave them some tools to facilitate team communication and conflict resolution.

- *Experiencing an intense, emotional, frame-breaking leadership "metaphor."* As in many Action Learning events, Shell used "breaking the frame" activities to force managers to think in new ways. They wanted to wake up and shake up participants. Going into the inner city and spending an afternoon working at a frontline human services AIDS clinic was a shared experience that was both memorable and effective as a team unifier. Issues such as internal obstacles, business goals, and resource limitations within their huge corporation suddenly paled in comparison and significance.

But do not think that Shell's leaders all bought into Action Learning from Day 1 of the first workshop. In fact, some actively resisted. They complained they had too many real priorities to waste their time on another initiative. Some of them resisted because the Action Learning format made them nervous or they felt that its style was not a useful way to learn (they preferred data presented by a recognized expert). The atmosphere during the workshop on the first day became confrontational and unpleasant. Unfortunately, because he was traveling in Asia, the CEO was unable to be a part of the first workshop. We ended the first night early and called him on the road. After briefing him on the resistance, he gave us a message to convey to participants: "This is important to me and the organization: Do it." After that, things went smoothly.

They went smoothly for reasons other than the CEO's message, however. As often happens, participants overcome their fears and concerns about Action Learning and become engaged in the process. After the first workshop, the Shell Oil leaders went off and engaged in research, interviewing, benchmarking, and analysis related to their projects. With the tools and ideas provided in the first workshop, they tackled significant issues as they attempted new ways to cut costs or raise revenues. They developed a sense of mission, recognizing that their work would impact the company's immediate bottom-line performance.

In both the strategic and operational workshops, Shell's leaders struggled as they worked and learned. One of the tougher things for them to deal with was working on a team of equals. Most team members were used to working in a hierarchy; they had to discuss and debate the issues of authority when it came to team decision making and assignments.

Still, the teams all made progress and had interim reports on their progress ready for the second workshop. During this second session, teams reported on what they had accomplished and received feedback from coaches, sponsors, and other teams. Shell found that having one team interview and critique another team had a positive impact. Not only is feedback more meaningful when coming from one's peers, but it helps each team realize that the problems they are experiencing are not unique—every team has them.

The feedback addressed questions such as

- Is your team on the right track?

- Will your project make a significant difference in cutting costs or raising revenues?

- Have you made any breakthroughs?

Feedback also revolved around process issues, such as how teams were working together and if conflicts were being resolved effectively. After the second workshop, teams moved forward on their projects, making course changes based on input received.

The third workshop involved teams making recommendations for implementation, and the executive committee decided whether to approve, reject, or ask for more information. Feedback and reflection were integral elements of this workshop. Team members had been together for a good portion of the last twelve weeks, and coaches asked them to provide each other with feedback about what people should do more of, do less of, or let stay the same. By the end of the workshop, a significant percentage of Shell's conservative, engineering-minded managers had learned to work and lead in a different way—a way that dovetailed with Shell's new performance-oriented direction.

A Temporary System

As you can see from these three examples, a certain degree of flexibility is built into Action Learning. Although teams are usually a component of the process, there are instances when participants work on an individual basis, such as coaching global partners at Arthur Andersen. Sometimes Action Learning is used primarily as a tool to achieve strategic business goals; other times, personal development of leaders is emphasized. In all cases, the focus is on a combination of personal development and business strategy. Some organizations pull their people out of their jobs so they can spend all their time on an Action Learning project; others perform their regular jobs and assume the new requirements of the program.

There are certain constants. Perhaps the most important one is the combination of *action* and *learning*. The three workshops (this number can vary) are the catalyst—coaches, professors, facilitators, sponsors, and others help participants acquire everything from fresh perspectives to innovative ideas. The time spent working on projects between workshops is the pure action phase—here the learning from the workshops is applied.

What Action Learning creates is a temporary system. It is a temporary environment that resembles the real world of work in many respects, but it is also one where people are free to take chances and fail without repercussions. They can try out new behaviors and ideas and take risks without fear of sanctions. What keeps all this from remaining "just" a learning exercise is that participants are held accountable for their (or their team's) performance. They are expected to produce viable recommendations that have a significant impact on the business. The tension between learning and action drives the process and makes it relevant and compelling.

While we will share other examples of Action Learning throughout this book, we want to stress that there is one element that always runs through the process. This element is difficult to describe in writing—you almost have to be there to get it—but it is critical. We refer to it as reflection, and it translates into all sorts of other words: self-analysis, contemplation, introspection, and plain thinking. We have found that one reason people in business do not change is that they do not take time to reflect. They do not have the space to think about "What am I learning and how does it apply to my own behavior? How do I adjust?"

There are opportunities for reflection throughout the Action Learning process. We encourage participants to think about everything from an eye-opening interview with a customer to critical feedback from a coach. This does not result, however, in an epiphany whereby a change-resistant manager suddenly becomes a change-embracing leader. By reflecting constantly, participants gradually begin to think and behave in new ways. Though we may not emphasize this point in each case history or anecdote about Action Learning, we want you to understand that time for reflection is always provided and reflection is always encouraged. Coaches, facilitators, and workshop leaders all encourage the application of learning through reflection on what is happening and why.

3

Why Change?

Rising to the Challenges of the New Business World

The title of this chapter poses a question that we have answered indirectly. From the examples in the last chapter, you have seen how organizations re-create leaders to become global, cross-functional thinkers. The impetus to do so is obvious: A global marketplace demands global leadership, and boundaryless organizations will not function effectively with people who manage from silos.

As obvious as these catalysts are, there are two, more subtle, issues involved:

- *The complexity, ambiguity, and paradoxical nature of the business environment,* to which traditional control-oriented type leaders are woefully unsuited. To adapt to this environment, leaders need to develop a range of new perspectives and behaviors.

- *The need for more homegrown leaders than ever before.* Decentralized, empowered organizations need leaders at all levels. Because recruiting all these new leaders is difficult (if not impossible), it is important to use a process to transform the people whom companies already have in place.

Let us briefly examine this second issue before moving on to the more problematic global business environment.

You Cannot Buy Love or Leadership

The very forces that are driving us to re-create our leaders make it difficult for us to purchase them. On the one hand, we need more leaders now than ever before. With decentralization, empowerment, and the need to be "planfully opportunistic" comes a need for leaders at all organizational levels. As a result, it is unlikely that any company can recruit enough leaders to circumvent the re-creating process. Even when this is possible, a company's culture often rejects the transplant.

More significantly, we cannot buy the right types of leaders for our particular organizations. Just because someone was in a leadership position with another company does not mean that he has been re-created; he may be nothing more than a new version of an old model. In addition, we are more likely to re-create leaders ourselves. Dealing with real business issues in a controlled environment is the path to re-creation. When people tackle *your* most challenging problems and opportunities in a learning-oriented situation is when new leaders emerge. In other words, they are re-created around your own business issues, not someone else's. Perhaps in the past there was an interchangeability of leadership. Today, most leaders emerge in response to specific situations and difficulties facing an organization—they are homegrown, not imported. Either this, or simply shipped off to a business school for a few weeks and dropped back into the culture.

Action Learning provides a process for do-it-yourself leadership re-creation. It is portable, adaptable, and relatively compressed. Most organizations can use it, no matter what traits they desire to develop in their emerging leaders. As we shall see, these traits are quite varied and relate directly to the specific business issues facing organizations. We refer to leaders on whom new learning has made an impact as "re-created leaders."

Leading Against the Grain

Jack Welch fixed something even though to most observers nothing was "broke." Phil Carroll said, "If this company waits for me to figure it out . . . we'll never get there." Bill Weiss was willing to encourage disagreement and abolish the tradition of pleasing the boss, even if it meant losing a number of top people.

The CEOs of General Electric, Shell Oil, and Ameritech are good examples of re-created leaders who have broken not only with their companies' traditions but with established leadership practices. They routinely reject the status quo, cede control, focus on a few key issues, and encourage debate and discussion. Yet if you think of the re-created leader only in terms of these four traits, you miss the point. While the old command-and-control-oriented leader might be easy to define, the new re-created leader is more amorphous. To paraphrase the poet Walt Whitman, this new leader contains and embraces contradictions. It would be convenient if we could describe new leaders as those who embrace change, think globally, and empower other employees. No question—these are important traits of re-created leaders. But like the times we live in, leadership is continuous and complex. From the ability to work well in ambiguous situations to an almost psychic sense of spotting markets before they appear, re-created leaders possess a wide range of attributes.

We want to give you a sense of what these attributes are and why they are so critical for every organization in every corner of the world.

Going to Extremes

There is no master list of traits that re-created leaders need. Or rather, there is a list but it contains more traits than anyone could ever possess. Though many of our clients have hoped to develop a set of leadership competencies through Action Learning—competencies that include global management skills, change agency, and team building, to name just a few—the targeted traits vary considerably and are often quite generic. Individual personality plays a role: One has to work on being more innovative and strategic in his thinking, whereas another has to focus on learning to work more effectively with different business units. In addition, targeted competencies are usually tied to the business problems or opportunities facing a company. One organization may be attempting to become a global player and wants to re-create its leaders with global management skills. Another organization may be struggling with diversity issues and needs its leadership to learn to manage a heterogeneous workforce or to embody new values.

Rather than offer a definitive list of traits that re-created leaders should possess, we would like to give you a sense of the shift in leadership "type" we are observing. Organizations are trying to develop people in very different ways than in the past; they are putting people into Action Learning with the hope that participants will shed outmoded leadership beliefs and behaviors and acquire fresh ideas and approaches.

To help you understand the shift and what is driving it, we have contrasted two extremes: a still prevalent, traditional command-and-control leadership model versus the emerging model driven by technology, globalization, and paradox. The following ten contrasting behaviors/mindsets illustrate the gaps between traditional leadership and re-created leadership:

- *Providing direction versus providing directions*. Leaders have often been detail-oriented and obsessed with checking, controlling, supervising, and correcting. Since technology flattened the pyramid and made information available to everyone instantly, there is no longer much need for a leader to control. The new leader has the freedom to look to the future, to strategize, inspire, and motivate. Re-created leaders are not frightened of this freedom; they do not fear that there will be less for them to do.

- *Owners versus managers.* In our Action Learning programs, we often ask participants, "If you, as a group, had participated in a management buyout of this business and mortgaged your house, your possessions, and all your net worth to make it successful, what would you be doing?" Re-created leaders think and act like business owners whereas traditional leaders think and act like managers—focusing on the short-term, currying favor with superiors, striving for seniority and security, decision making phlegmatically, plodding through an endless series of internal processes. Ownership became a leadership imperative as organizations recognized the importance of adding value, and the bureaucratic mentality did nothing to add value. Companies are striving to create ownership with wider grants of stock and performance incentives.

- *What might be versus what is.* There is no longer much advantage in being as good as or even a bit better than the competition. This is a radical thought for executives brought up in cultures in which incremental gains were prized and the bottom line was holy. Leaders need to be re-created in such a way that they unlock information and knowledge from new places; they must help their people discover new markets and new customers and have the flexibility to "turn on a dime" dramatically. Organizations are competing against themselves—the real competitive advantage is gained when one redefines one's market. We have watched Microsoft redefine its strategy in a business nanosecond and Johnson & Johnson enter and exit business overnight.

- *Involvement versus isolation*. For traditional leaders, it really *is* lonely at the top. People report to them, but no one communicates in a free-flowing, interactive way. An article in the June 24, 1997 issue of *Fortune* cited consultant Richard Hagberg's study of 511 CEOS with its conclusion that many of them remain "egocentric," "individualistic," and "loners." CEOs will need to become leaders who meet regularly with business heads, share information, and seek feedback—negative as well as positive. Jack Welch at G.E. certainly has been a model for this re-created leader quality by encouraging an open dialogue, despite potential difficulties.

- *Generalist versus functionalist*. Much has been said and written about the need to get people to work cross-functionally, but even the leaders who endorse this view are often constricted by their functional upbringing. In most companies today, leaders are known for what they do, for their specific functional expertise. To forsake that function and broaden one's view is psychologically difficult. One of the most challenging tasks in our Action Learning programs is helping people achieve a general management perspective. Though rotating people through functions helps achieve this objective, it is a very slow and not always effective process. Re-created leaders do not just experience different functions, they learn to see the interdependencies between functions. A great challenge and risk a company endures is when a functional leader becomes CEO—often this is the first time he is called upon to lead as a generalist, and it is a difficult transition. Re-created leaders learn to think and work as generalists before becoming CEOs.

- *Reflection versus doing.* Traditional leaders are often defined by perpetual activity—generating transactions, inspecting sites, acquiring, divesting, attending meetings, doing deals, walking the factory floor. Good leaders get things done, but they also make and take time to reflect. This is not an indulgence but a necessity. Analysis will only take you so far in an age of ambiguity and paradox. Leaders need to develop their intuitive sense, and that can best be achieved through reflection. Sometimes you have to sense when it is time to make a move (rather than analyze mounds of data), and re-created leaders use this sixth sense and value it.

- *Emotion versus intellect.* Re-created leaders produce emotional energy—energy that motivates their people to sign up and commit. Teams run on this energy and accomplish great things because of it. Leaders can mobilize people who may not even report directly to them but who are galvanized by their energy, point of view, and passion. All this is in contrast to analytical, coolly detached, or even imperious leaders, who may inspire obedience and even respect but do not get people excited.

- *Faith versus skepticism.* Traditional leaders check everything twice, leaving nothing to chance. Many of them are firm believers in Murphy's Law—if something can go wrong, it will go wrong—and so they constantly check up on people to make sure they are doing their jobs properly. Re-created leaders maintain a high trust level. At a time when speed is critical and people are located all over the globe, leaders need to trust those they work with, especially in leading virtual teams. It is impossible to control subordinates on the other side of the world or suppliers or partners who have to move with great speed. Re-created leaders do not waste time constantly monitoring the actions of others; they find and work with people who share their sense of trust and commitment.

- *Receptive versus rejecting*. There is a certain truth to the stereotype of the tough-minded leader whose every look and gesture says, "Prove it to me." Control-oriented leaders took pride in their ability to say no, to reject ideas and actions that did not measure up to their standards. They also rejected people who were not their type of people (and embraced those who were—the old boy network syndrome). It is still not unusual to see a top management team who all look, act, speak, and think in similar ways. Re-created leaders are highly receptive to ideas and people that are different from their own; they judge them on their merits alone. They relish the concept of diversity and do not turn their back on an idea just because it is unusual or off-the-wall. They seek out the new, the young, the original, or even the bizarre in order to keep in touch and stay on the edge.

- *Free speech versus censorship*. In traditional bureaucracies, people place conscious and unconscious limits on what they say and what they are willing to hear. Today, there are still leaders who withhold information from people, soften criticism of superiors, intimidate subordinates (thereby limiting what subordinates were willing to reveal), and attempt to "get along" with anyone who might do them harm. Re-created leaders recognize that clear and honest communication is essential; dealing with complex, ambiguous issues is tough if information is distorted or missing.

For this reason, leaders must be open to giving and getting feedback—negative or positive. They recognize that they must continually adjust their positions based on new information, and a steady stream of feedback helps them do so. Cycle time now demands dealing with conflict openly and constructively.

Is Re-Creating Really Required?

For people to consciously change their leadership behaviors is sometimes frightening and overwhelming. Seriously and sincerely trying change suggests an act of almost biblical proportions ("almost" because most Action Learning programs take more than a week, minus one day for resting, of course). Perhaps there is a more moderate alternative than starting from scratch and rebuilding. Instead of a full makeover, why not opt for a little, selective, cosmetic surgery?

Why not? Because that is what we have been doing and it has not worked. Executive development programs, internal to both corporation and university structures, are designed to help managers become change agents, think globally, and value diversity. Although a few programs may help achieve these goals, many do not. Learning to embrace change is not something learned overnight or through listening to change gurus lecture. It requires an experience that is emotional as well as intellectual; it demands feedback and confrontation and reflection. Beyond that, many companies have failed to realize that there is no magic key to leadership. It simply does not work to embrace the latest leadership trend, from quality improvement to effective habits, enroll hundreds of people, and expect to influence behavior and create cultural change. Focusing on helping people acquire special traits is not enough; the traits actually required are many and varied. Nothing less than a systematic focus that supports the new traits has an impact.

What is driving us to metamorphose our leaders? We all know the major forces impacting organizations today—forces such as globalization, technology, change, and growth. But let's look at those forces from a leadership perspective and how they are shaping completely new goals.

Technology, for instance, is driving leaders to learn a new form of communication. The old form was a laborious process of memos, letters, phone calls, and meetings in which information was passed back and forth (though not always to the right people at the right time). Leaders managed this information flow, and doing so required a great deal of time. Computer technology gives people instant access to most information, thus rendering the function of information management obsolete. But it has also given rise to a new communication imperative: connecting people to the big picture. How can one individual in a function such as accounting contribute to the company's overall goals? How can someone in product development use her information to influence the company's long-range strategy? The challenge for emerging leaders is to plug people into big organizational goals, defining their roles within the larger scheme of things.

Although most executives acknowledge the need to think globally, many of them have not translated thought into action. Consider that leaders in both big and small companies need to learn how to adapt constantly to people from different national cultures—cultures in which the assumptions for time, space, ethics, formality, and deal-making are different and often unconscious. This is a tremendous challenge for many people.

When we started Action Learning programs at G.E., we discovered that there were some U.S. executives who had never traveled outside of the country! New leaders need to learn skills of adaptation and acceptance—no easy task—but they must also learn about themselves and how their cultural assumptions continuously affect how they view (and judge) others. We have found that it is most effective to hold Action Learning sessions in various foreign countries and have participants experience and reflect upon the issues raised by working in those cultures.

Change in all its forms is another catalyst for re-creating our leaders. More than anything else, it has turned traditional viewpoints and practices into anachronisms. Leaders now need to think and act in untraditional ways, and for many leaders, nothing is harder. Too many top executives are still uncomfortable dealing with representatives of the "wired world" who dress and act in "unbusinesslike" ways. The concepts of meditation and reflection as tools to problem-solve also strike some as weird and inappropriate. We are not advocating oddness for oddness' sake, but simply saying that re-created leaders are open to new sources of competitive advantage. They cannot afford to shut out anyone because they are not high enough in the organization or to reject ideas because they are not in line with conventional wisdom. The notion of "planful opportunism" means discovering knowledge and information about the competition and the customer at every level, and re-created leaders embrace this notion. They know long-range planning is truly impossible. The goal is to plan continuously to be ready.

Leaders who emerge in the next ten years will be far more flexible than those of the past. In a world of constant change, flexibility is crucial. We will need to train leaders to challenge everything—their processes, their theories, and their assumptions. Until recently, companies had the luxury of trusting implicitly in their success. In every industry—computers, telecommunication, retailing, manufacturing—are examples of great companies and strong leaders who made the fundamental error of assuming that the future would look like the present. IBM, Sears, AT&T, Kodak, all great companies, have had to jump painfully onto new growth curves late in their previous success cycles. "Whom the gods wish to destroy, they send thirty years of success." Now we need to think: If it ain't broke, it soon may be. Why did IBM find it difficult to challenge its business strategy, but Microsoft did not? Companies often fall in love with a strategy or process and cannot distinguish the environmental signals that something is changing. Such signals are often weak at first and difficult to discern. They usually appear at the margins—a product is not selling as well; a new technology has appeared; the customers' own strategies are changing. Future leaders will develop an evolved auditory sense—the equivalent of a Darwinian survival instinct—that is attuned to those signals.

Then there is growth to consider. It is not just that business must grow but how that growth is happening that has an impact on leaders' roles. Alliances, networks, partnerships, and all manner of collaborations now make leadership a much more complex task. What happens when you are collaborating with a competitor in one area and competing fiercely against them in another? How do you secure commitment to a common goal when your alliance partners have such diverse agendas? How can you possibly partner with a company whose culture is so different from your own? Unless leaders transform their ideas and behaviors, these tasks are difficult.

Someone Has to Drive the Process

If you are going to re-create your leaders, you need a strong commitment to the process. It can be volatile, and people might get "hurt." At Ameritech, Action Learning was used to reshape both the business strategy and structure. As a result of the restructuring, a number of top executives resigned because they were unable or unwilling to sign up to what the others were demanding. We cannot overemphasize the importance of a strong sponsor. Without the firm support of Ameritech's chairman Bill Weiss, the process would have been stopped by the inevitable resistance. We do not say this to frighten anyone; many times we have run Action Learning programs that did not result in the loss of a single executive. Still, Action Learning can unleash core debates that can create fear, and whether the danger is real or imagined, the end result is resistance to the process. Some people hate the thought of having to learn or change, and they simply believe that they are right and refuse to challenge their beliefs.

Given anticipated resistance, there must be someone at or near the top of the organization to drive the process. Jack Welch did this at G.E. in a very charismatic way, but it can also be done quietly and just as effectively.

Many times, top executives get behind this concept and drive it because they have seen that it has worked wonders elsewhere. Ameritech's Action Learning program was inspired by G.E.'s; Shell Oil's was inspired by Ameritech's. Johnson & Johnson was inspired by both of these companies. Benchmarking is a powerful motivator in every area, including leadership.

Sometimes the way to secure a CEO's support is by starting small. In fact, most organizations do not start out trying to change hundreds of leaders. Some begin with a small test group to see how and if the process works. Others do not even aim as high as leadership, and instead use Action Learning to help solve a specific problem or seize a specific opportunity—Company X wants to help a group of managers in R&D learn to come up with new, more innovative concepts as a result of technological changes in their industry.

One way or another, someone has to lead this effort. If support is lukewarm or the sponsor is someone without much clout, the odds are that few if any leaders will be influenced.

Crisis as Catalyst

Crisis clearly spurs management to action. The specter of plummeting profits and other calamitous events prompts organizations to assess their leadership capabilities. It causes them to question whether they have the right people with the right vision in place, given changes in the marketplace. Crisis catalyzes management and, if focused, inspires action.

Ameritech, for instance, was a regulated monopoly that became a more competitive, market-driven business through Action Learning. Increasing competition and telecommunication reform has affected virtually every aspect of Ameritech, including and especially the culture. In 1991, environmental changes drove the company and especially Chairman Bill Weiss to embrace Action

Learning, hoping it would help them define a vision for the organization's future with an eye toward providing new leadership. The gathering storm was evident, as was the fact that traditional executive development could not quickly and radically influence hundreds of leaders.

We began working with 120 "change agents" drawn from all levels of the company. Though they were all different from one another in many respects, what they had in common was an ability to get things done and a reputation for being nontraditional. They were selected by a "lead team" of similar change agents—junior level executives below the executive committee charged to spearhead the Action Learning events. We put them through an Action Learning process that entailed a series of workshops in which they learned team skills, were placed in demanding situations, had to meet an outdoor challenge, and made specific recommendations about key issues facing the company.

Based on these workshops, Bill Weiss was able to select his successor, Dick Notebaert, from the lead team. Just as important, the process helped provide Ameritech with a cadre of leaders, leaving some behind as well. In the old regulated monopoly, leadership revolved around the internal politics of survival and pleasing the boss—characteristics of the Bell system. Customers were considered a necessary evil but not one to be overly concerned about—where else could the customers go? Back then, leaders had little understanding of the business engine and what produced growth and profit, and "revenue requirements" could be presented to regulators without the nasty distractions of competition.

The new leaders, on the other hand, understood the business drivers intimately. Each could identify not only what drove value in their particular business area but for the company as a whole. They were committed to winning and serving customers, and they had acquired a diverse group of tools that helped them manage teams, reduce cycle time, and improve processes.

Citibank, too, turned to Action Learning in response to a crisis. In 1991, the organization went through a difficult experience because of bad real estate investments and loans to Latin American companies. Though CEO John Reed managed the company out of its crisis spectacularly, he also recognized that he needed to focus on strengthening Citibank's management team. From the near-death experience, he recognized the technological and competitive forces that would reshape the financial industry in the coming decade. To deal with these forces, leaders will have to find and grow new markets (even if they are not "visible" at first glance), manage to a higher performance level, and take the costs out of the existing structure. Reed was well aware that many of Citibank's leaders reacted to the turnaround passively—they preferred to manage as though nothing had changed, albeit after uttering a sigh of relief for their good fortune. To avoid another business crisis, Citibank is attempting to re-create the company's leaders.

Can People Re-Create Themselves?

Action Learning simply gives an organization a tool to help transform its leaders. It does not guarantee transformation, and we have found that some participants strongly resist changing their attitudes and behaviors. Ultimately, it is up to the individual as to whether the process is successful. Over the years, we have been heartened by how adaptable and open-minded most people are. Although some enter Action Learning skeptical and even hostile, most emerge with an appreciation for the process and new perspectives and skills. Just as important, they evolve into leaders who are more attuned to the requirements and business goals of their organizations.

Is it possible for leaders in a company to re-create themselves? What are the odds that Action Learning will work for your company? Start out by determining whether your company has the advantage of possessing the following four factors:

- *A top-down commitment to learning, change, and challenge.* The more people at the top of the organization who genuinely support the process of learning, the better. We have found that our Action Learning programs achieve real results when people in the top are participants rather than spectators—they are willing to challenge their own assumptions and re-create themselves if need be, serving as models for others. The chances of success are lessened when top people remove themselves from the "action" or fail to fund and facilitate the process.

- *An avoidance of the faddish and the superficial.* Some companies attempt to re-create their leaders superficially. Management wants to portray themselves as being on the "cutting edge," embracing techniques that purport to re-engineer, transform, and change but do not. These techniques are like diet drugs—they sound great but leave you in no better shape than before, and are potentially dangerous.

- *Cultures that encourage openness and a spirit of discovery.* Some cultures are highly political; others are burdened with silo mentalities; still others are locked into traditional practices, or are highly critical and control-oriented. You cannot expect many people to develop truly different skills and attitudes in strong cultures. It is amazing how often companies fail to practice what they preach. They may want their leaders to work and manage cross-functionally, but the reality of their corporate life is that marketing and manufacturing may have the same amount of trust in each other as Israel and the PLO.

- *Human resources buys in to, supports, and is capable of having an impact on the re-creating process.* This is not always the case. Many times HR views Action Learning as threatening to its role, power, or position; it is threatened with the loss of control and sabotage the effort. In these situations, it fails to redesign recruiting, compensation, and performance management systems to reinforce the new, desired leadership traits, or subtly undermine the role of outsiders.

You Don't Have to Be Greek to Have Hubris

You may remember *hubris* from studying Greek tragedy. Quickly defined, hubris means excessive pride. Translated into a business environment, it means a belief that one can do no wrong; that the current way is, by definition, the right way; that success can be counted on to beget more success.

Again, there is a certain merit to this argument for organizations in years past. Market leaders in many industries had a stranglehold on their markets, and to a certain extent, their hubris was justified.

Today, however, things change with astonishing speed. If we are not flexible, self-reflective, and humble, we will get blindsided—unforeseen competition and technological breakthroughs have a way of catching arrogant companies unaware. The best example of this is IBM, of course, which spent millions on training and developing their leaders. Unfortunately, they were training and developing them in the IBM way, a way unconsciously fostered by the belief that they could control success in the future in the way it has controlled it in the past. IBM was the model for traditional executive development—one that many companies still emulate today, even after IBM has abandoned it.

In Action Learning, we teach a company's prospective leaders to be afraid and to anticipate failure. These are not tenets of which many companies would approve, yet they are at the heart of what is driving new leaders. Change strikes with such speed, growth is such an overwhelming imperative, global markets appear and disappear almost magically, and technology humbles us all. In this environment, to not be afraid of what is going to happen next or to believe that our success makes us impervious to failure is foolhardy. Still, at the top of the pyramid it does not seem this clear.

Of course, we have all been trained otherwise and cannot untrain ourselves. In Action Learning, when we re-create leadership, we do not simply put people in a classroom and teach them about fear and failure. As you shall see, we need to let them experience it.

Part Two

Putting Action Learning to Work

4

You Can't Buy Leadership
Transforming Leaders in Place

Action Learning is not the only leadership program in the world. All types of executive development programs, business school courses, and guru-led workshops purport to be the sine qua non of leadership training. Why is Action Learning better?

It is not better, but it is different. *Better* implies that we have hit upon some magic formula, and that is not the case. Unlike other methods, however, Action Learning is integrative—it delivers a cognitive, emotional, and business-focused experience. If you want to recreate someone—if you need to change how an individual views the world and acts in it—you must address the whole person. Other approaches address different pieces of the whole. Action Learning may borrow techniques and tools from other leadership disciplines, but it is unique in the way it influences people from many directions and on multiple levels; it provides a milieu in which transformation is possible.

Still, given all the competing leadership programs and processes, taking the above paragraphs on faith is difficult. Let us look at how organizations train leaders formally and informally and discover why these methods are incapable of achieving the higher goal of leadership re-creation.

The Informal Methods

CEOs like to think that their people will acquire leadership skills on the job. The predominant metaphor in business is still "the cream will rise to the top." To a certain extent, on-the-job training works best, especially if a business is growing or changing quickly. In these circumstances, many new situations present themselves and the opportunity exists to observe and test different behaviors and skills. In most organizations, however, people repeat behaviors and skills ad infinitum because the culture elicits conformity. The intellectual challenge and emotional component needed to re-create are missing. Although you can pick up certain old paradigm leadership skills by observing and doing, it is tough to learn one's own capabilities, point of view, and personal limits in this way.

Another informal method of leadership training relies on relationships with other people—bosses, mentors, coaches. Certainly you can pick up leadership competencies under the tutelage of wise people and good role models. But no matter how much wisdom another person has, he or she does not have the power to transform through wisdom alone. We assume there are some excellent coaches out there who have an inordinate amount of influence, and perhaps they can re-create their charges, but this is the exception. Besides, the people most likely to acquire the services of mentors and coaches are an organization's more junior people; they are not always in key leadership positions. In fact, by the time a person achieves a senior leadership role, quite often their formal leadership development has stopped. They are not mentored, they do not participate in outside programs, and they are too time-pressed to reflect or even read. In addition, many organizational leaders are reluctant to provide others with any type of negative feedback for legal and other reasons, so their coaching does not have much of an emotional impact.

Certainly there are many informal methods by which a leader might re-create herself. A mid-life crisis, getting fired, a work epiphany or some serious soul-searching might catalyze someone to become a different type of leader. Most companies, however, cannot depend on random epiphanies for their next generation of leadership.

Formal Methods

Leadership approaches and techniques abound, but for the sake of analysis, let us look at them within the context of the following five broad categories:

- *Gurus.* The idea here is to adopt a leadership expert and attempt to translate his lessons to your circumstances. Organizations routinely bring in these gurus for workshops and lectures; they urge people to read their books and they devise workbooks and other tools to help translate these lessons in leadership into real work-life skills. The problem is not that these gurus do not have worthwhile things to say, or that they do not communicate their lessons well. Not to offend anyone, but the best analogy is with a religious leader. The minister gets up on the pulpit and delivers an eloquent and moving sermon on greed. Many in the congregation vow then and there to change their ways and become more altruistic and less focused on making money. The majority of those who made that vow, however, will forsake it the next day or the next week. The impact of most gurus is short-term. Unless a legion of gurus is onsite and working with people for a sustained period, they will not accomplish much genuine change.

- *Executive education/business school model.* When it comes to imparting "hard" general management skills, this can be an effective process. With use of case studies of best-practice companies, this method helps future leaders learn a range of functional skills. When it comes to the "soft" skills we discussed in the last chapter—learning to become owners, provide direction, and so on—it is largely irrelevant. Cognitive, case-based teaching does not require people to take risks or deal with real issues facing their companies. Participants, like students, are passive observers of entertaining speakers (who receive excellent evaluations because of the entertainment they provide), dealing in theory and abstract concepts. There is another problem with the executive education model: Its teachings are not sustained in the work environment. If you have ever been in an executive education program, you have heard people say, "I really wish my boss was here." People wish this because once they return to work, no one is reinforcing the lessons learned or giving them the opportunity to apply what they have learned.

- *Outdoor adventures*. To encourage team building, communication, and other soft skills that are now in great demand, organizations have used Outward Bound–type experiences such as rafting rivers, climbing mountains, building bridges, and so on. With the right structure and facilitation, these experiences can contribute to the re-creating process. They can be emotionally charged, involve risk, and take participants out of familiar environments. On the other hand, many people have difficulty making the connection between surviving in the wilderness and surviving in the global marketplace. Expecting a non-business experience to transform the way people look at business is unreasonable. Although we use these methods selectively in Action Learning programs, they are seldom effective as stand-alone interventions.

- *Behavior-based programs.* To re-create leaders, we need to change behaviors. The Center for Creative Leadership and other groups have recognized this truth and developed programs to change leadership. For instance, 360-degree feedback involves comments and constructive criticism from peers, subordinates, and superiors. The idea is to identify behaviors in need of change and work with a coach who might facilitate this change. Such a process might help a prospective leader recognize that she is a control freak and needs to develop a strategy for "letting go" of some assignments. As critical as new behaviors are for re-creating leadership, if they are not linked to key business issues, they often improve the person without improving his impact on the business.

- *Lateral or developmental assignments.* The theory is that leaders have to learn new skills and roles, and they will do so if they are taken out of familiar jobs, departments, and offices and placed in unfamiliar ones. This often means rotating people into jobs and geographies that are highly challenging and lack the usual support systems, thus providing prospective leaders with valuable new perspectives and learning. Again, we believe this concept has significant value, but it is not a panacea. As good as it is for helping future leaders break out of their silos, it does not take people out of their cultural assumptions and expose them to new ideas and risks. Transportation does not equal transformation.

The Skills Re-Created Leaders Need . . . and Do Not Learn

Ideally, future leaders will be exposed to one of the leadership techniques described in the previous section (ideally, of course, they should be exposed to all of them). But the odds are that even if they are exposed, the lessons will not hit home or have a lasting effect. As leaders rise in the hierarchy, they are still caught in functional webs. Their ascension to new leadership roles rests on their ability to satisfy a functional boss or master functional skills. The chance to develop a systems view of the business and its concomitant big picture perspective is often limited.

A new generation of leadership finds itself lacking the new skills critical in a complex global environment. We have talked about some of these skills in a general sense—global thinking; the ability to manage in a complex, ambiguous world; being comfortable with change; working cross-functionally; and managing diversity—but there is a wide variety of more specific skills that flow from these general ones. Although the leadership skills required by a given leader vary from company to company, the following will give you a sense of their distinctiveness and the difficulty of acquiring them through traditional executive development:

- *The ability to compete "on time."* Traditional leaders focus their competitive efforts on cost and quality factors. Though these remain important, re-created leaders are skilled at time-based competition. Now, being the first to market is paramount, and it takes a certain type of leader to take the risks and roll the dice this way. Managing rapid product cycles is another component in this skill category—driving a product from engineering to manufacturing to marketing requires an ability to deal with complexity quickly.

- *Working flexibly.* In modern organizations, rules change routinely and reporting relationships become ambiguous. Boundaryless organizations tear down external and internal barriers, and leadership must be comfortable working with all types of people in all types of teams, including virtual teams that cut across geography and function. One way or another, new leaders must get rigidity out of their systems.

- *A breakthrough mentality.* This is as opposed to the incremental mentality of many traditional leaders. It is much easier and safer to make incremental improvements and avoid the risk and dramatic change of breakthroughs. Re-created leaders ignite breakthrough ideas in product development, applications, systems, and people.

- *Lean/stretch capacity.* Although many leaders are good at cutting costs, they are not so good at controlling them. A lean/stretch environment—resources applied leanly to achieve stretch goals—makes many managers uncomfortable. Most people need to be re-created before they feel comfortable setting highly ambitious goals or seeing the path to reach them while lacking plentiful resources to achieve them.

- *Managing the new employee relationship.* The essence of this relationship is the psychological reward of winning, rather than the guarantee of employment. To mobilize and motivate, re-created leaders draw on this reward. They have inculcated this psychology, and their people respond to it.

- *Knowing one's self.* This last skill may seem too soft for hardcore managers, but that is precisely why people need to be re-created to appreciate it. In the new business paradigm, leaders must possess insight about their strengths and weaknesses; they must be able to reflect about their intentions, self-manage stress, and recharge themselves when they are running low on energy. Lack of self-awareness today can jeopardize projects faster and more surely than in the past—we no longer can

give leaders the latitude to operate at less than peak
efficiency (not to mention crashing and burning in the
middle of a project, or widely disseminating personal
stress and anxiety to others).

The Magic of Re-Creation: Secrets Revealed

Skepticism is understandable—refusing to believe that people in
your organization can acquire the skills just described; that a
control-oriented leader can change into a delegator; that an inflexible manager can become an open-minded one. Having seen thousands of leaders impacted, we obviously are believers. There is
nothing like witnessing the process to make a believer out of you.

Throughout this book, we give you examples of this process,
demonstrating that even the most resistant individual can be influenced. Here, our goal is to share some of our approaches behind the
process. It is always a bit easier to believe that something is possible when we have a better understanding of how something works.
Let us start with a principle that should be self-evident but is not:

*Re-creating does not happen by waving a wand or uttering magic
words.*

Or to state this another way,

Re-creating is reliant on many factors, not just one key catalyst.

Executive development programs cannot change the way a
future leader thinks and acts by focusing on a single aspect of that
person. People do not change through cognitive approaches that
are purely intellectual or analytical, and leaders do not change
through team-based approaches that concentrate only on group
skills, or through risk-taking activities that give one's emotions a
good workout but fail to build business acumen.

One quality that differentiates our Action Learning programs from others is that it is learning for the whole person (as opposed to learning for the intellectual, emotional, or business part). When the whole person is involved, transformation becomes possible. When we are fully engaged in a process, we are much more likely to be profoundly influenced by it. It is very difficult for people to "hide out" or rely on their traditional strengths in Action Learning. The process forces people to test new behaviors and ideas; it confronts them with their weaknesses and who they are as managers and leaders and helps them to understand the future needs of the business.

Perhaps more than other companies, Ameritech illustrates the dramatic nature of re-creation and transition. When we began their Action Learning program, we found many managers resistant to changing the culture of a regulated, secure telephone company. Not only did they resist the notion of becoming highly competitive leaders, they had difficulty accepting the reality of that competition. They were not comfortable with ambiguity and complexity! Ameritech's managers were traditional leaders through and through; they were like heads of a country that had lived in blissful isolation for years and suddenly were being forced to join the international community.

Yet Ameritech's leaders changed, albeit not overnight. After some initial resistance, they entered a "discovery" phase in which they absorbed a great deal of new information. Then they went through a "struggling" phase in which they worked in teams to integrate new ideas and formulate new behaviors and concepts; they faced all sorts of intellectual and emotional challenges related to significant issues facing Ameritech. Finally, they went through an "assimilation" phase in which they reflected on their experiences, received feedback, and allowed new ideas and behaviors to sink in and become part of them. Though not every single one of Ameritech's participants was successfully re-created, a significant percentage were radically changed during the process.

If you recall the elements of the process described in the first chapter and the case histories we related in the second chapter, you

may have a sense of Action Learning's gestalt. The range of experiences and ideas combined with the interpersonal intensity make
it unlike any developed experience participants have ever
attempted. One day people may be rafting a river and the next
working with their team on a challenging business project. They
may be interviewing customers, benchmarking companies, receiving feedback on their performance from coaches and team members, and reflecting on everything that has taken place. All this
confuses people, pushes them to the limit, energizes and excites
them. The pressure, new experiences, and unpredictability that
mark many of the sessions help people question their beliefs and
behaviors in a way no other type of training can.

Why do participants not crack under the pressure? Or why do
they even take the process seriously? The answer to both questions
is that Action Learning provides people with the "cushion" of a
temporary system, a virtual business world that resembles the workplace but also is removed from it. They are often grouped in teams,
but the teams are far more heterogeneous than anything they are
used to. They are assigned real business projects, but the projects
often are more strategic in nature and more challenging than what
they have dealt with in the past. They alternate work on projects
with personal feedback, risk-taking, and other non-work activities.
Coaches and facilitators also influence the direction of the program
and provide tools and advice (unlike the real work environment).
They encourage people to try new behaviors and ideas, and they
guide the process. As a result of all this, participants are given every
opportunity to develop and exhibit the qualities of recreated leaders.

Increasing the Odds of Transforming People Effectively

This process of re-creation does not work smoothly every time.
Action Learning works better in some organizations than others.
Though you cannot control all the factors that determine a program's

effectiveness, you can control many of them. Let us look at some of the factors that you should consider when setting up a program:

- A *clear process and reason to re-create*. In terms of the latter, people are much more likely to want to transform themselves if they understand a clear business case or rationale and see the benefits to themselves and their organizations. In terms of the former, they are much more willing to embark on this uncertain leadership journey if they understand how they are going to get to their destination. Action Learning provides a framework or process for transformation—it is orderly, organized, and tested. You probably can find another process or framework to use, so Action Learning is not the only way. We just want to emphasize the importance of a framework for change that will give people the step-by-step assurance that the process is purposeful.

- *Career stage openness*. Some of us are more receptive to re-creation than others. If we have experienced the failure of the old leadership model in a direct way, we may be more open to a new model. We may also be going through a personal change, such as mid-life or some other emotional stage that prompts us to be more willing to think and act differently.

- *Emotional engagement*. We have said it before and we will say it again: No one is going to be transformed who is not emotionally plugged-in. You have to feel badly that your current course resulted in a negative or at least nonproductive outcome and feel exhilarated when new actions provided a fresh approach.

- *Reinforcement*. Ideally, the re-creating process will not be confined to a handful of people during a limited time frame. When people return to their real jobs, it is critical to provide tools and other forms of support that reinforce how and why they were re-created. The redesign of the organizational system, such as compensation, staffing, and management practices, is essential to the reinforcement of the re-creation.

Actions and Learnings

Let us stop for a moment and do a reality check. Most of you reading this are probably attempting to figure out where your company stands on these issues. You naturally have thought about which leadership training programs your company subscribes to and whether your people have some of the skills of re-created leaders. To help you to make this determination, ask yourself the following questions:

1. *Do you rely exclusively or to a large extent on case-based teaching and outside experts?* Case histories considered "best practice" are often irrelevant or difficult to apply to a specific situation because of differences in organizational culture, industry, history, or business context. Sometimes they are simply anachronisms used because they are considered classic cases.

2. *Is cognitive learning given far more weight than emotional or behavioral experimentation and change?* In other words, leaders are expected to learn with their minds and are not expected to become more self-aware and able to assess/change behaviors.

3. *Is there a direct link between your leadership development strategy and business strategy?* Stimulating leaders with brilliant ideas in the executive development process is one thing, and applying those ideas to the requirements and direction of the business is quite another. When you re-create leaders, you link everything to real business issues.

4. *Do your future leaders risk anything real during their training?* Are they accountable with real consequences for what they do during their training experience? Do senior executives get involved and judge what they have learned and how they have applied it? Are people's careers affected by their performance in a leadership training program? These questions will help you determine whether anything is really at stake.

5. *Are reflection and feedback part of the process?* If people are going to change their traditional practices and behaviors, they need to be given the opportunity to reflect on a wide range of meaningful feedback. Without it, there is just lip service to changing leadership style and substance.

6. *Is any effort made to help prospective leaders break out of their functional silos?* The key here is that the training process subverts the system; it encourages a broader view of the business.

7. *Is your succession planning designed to make smooth transitions?* Or is it designed to take chances on people who might shake up the system and help the company take big steps forward rather than smaller, incremental ones?

8. *Do you do equal-opportunity coaching?* In other words, coaching is not reserved for special people or problem-employees. Coaching is essential for re-creating leadership. No-pulled-punches feedback is what helps leaders discard outmoded behaviors and develop productive new ones.

5

Growing Global Leaders

L et us say you are with a company with grand global aspirations setting up offices in South America, Europe, and the Pacific Rim countries. You are shipping your top domestic people all over the world in an effort to get your new offices up and running. Unfortunately, your people are having problems, especially in places like Manila and Bogota, which are worlds apart from what is familiar to Northwestern University and Harvard University M.B.A.'s raised in Omaha and Providence. Some of them are finding working on teams with their foreign counterparts impossible. Other take-charge managers are frustrated with how long it takes to "get something done over here." Still others find reconciling corporate policies with local market realities difficult if not impossible.

Clearly, you need to find a better way to prepare your people for becoming part of the global community. The problem is that nothing seems to work or at least everything seems to have serious drawbacks. You can train people in the language, customs, and business etiquette of foreign countries and hope that eases the transition. You can make their work easier by allowing them to ignore corporate strategy and policy, giving them the latitude necessary to do business the local way.

As you will see throughout this chapter, none of these approaches is satisfactory, because they fail to confer a key skill that all global managers must have:

The ability to create trusting relationships across boundaries, to do so
quickly, and to maintain them.

Action Learning, however, is amazingly adept at helping all sorts of
business people acquire this skill.

Bringing Good Things to Life in Bombay and Other Places

When Jack Welch joined General Electric in the 1980s, about 18 percent of their business was international. Today that figure is 40 percent and quickly moving to the 50 percent range. Without Action
Learning, this dramatic success might not have been possible.

The bright idea to apply Action Learning to global leadership
issues did not come out of the blue. It was a natural evolution and
a response to a need. Originally, Welch had used Action Learning
to transform domestic leadership, attempting to get his people more
customer-focused. That effort had been highly successful, but by the
mid–1980s, it was clear that the customer battle was shifting in a
global direction. Not only were G.E.'s global markets such as power
systems, lighting, appliances, and medical imagery heating up, but
global competitors such as Phillips and Toshiba were making inroads
in the United States

At the behest of international vice president Paolo Fresco,
whose call for people to "think with global brains" was being
heard, G.E. began taking its Action Learning abroad. As much
faith as G.E. had in Action Learning, they knew that it was an
uphill climb to achieve the ideal "trust across boundaries." Many
of their key executives had little international experience. Beyond
all that they did not know about doing business in other countries,
they often lacked the ability to establish productive relationships
with people who acted, talked, worked, and thought in very different ways.

In one Action Learning session, for example, a team of Americans and Japanese were frustrated because they could not come up with a viable recommendation. An American executive accused one of the Japanese team members of "just sitting there and not making a contribution." The Japanese individual responded that it would be easier to contribute if the Americans did not "dominate the conversation with meaningless chatter and allowed everyone the silence necessary to think."

The obstacles to global leadership go beyond this example, of course. We use it only to suggest that G.E., or Johnson & Johnson, or Arthur Andersen (or any company, for that matter) has to overcome more than a lack of knowledge or skills if it wants to produce a new type of global leader. Let us focus on one Action Learning program to see how G.E. did it.

It began with an executive development course in 1991 in Heidelberg, Germany (G.E. had long since realized that global Action Learning programs needed to be conducted in targeted countries rather than in Crotonville, G.E.'s management development center). The need to have global leaders in this area was especially acute, as G.E. did not have a strong presence in Germany whereas its major international competitors did.

The Action Learning program we are about to describe takes place over a period of four weeks. Detailing all the dramatic interactions, turning points, and internal transformations is simply impossible. Sometimes, in our descriptions of these events, we focus on individuals and how they changed. Here, we give you an overview of the process and how it has an impact on the whole person (not just the business part or the team part).

The program began by introducing the group to G.E.'s Leadership Effectiveness Survey (LES), a hard-hitting feedback tool linked to corporate values. After a top executive shared his LES results and explained how it helped him improve his global leadership abilities, each participant received their own LES feedback. They then had access to coaching and also discussed the feedback after they broke into project teams.

This is not dry stuff. Sometimes the feedback creates surprise dissonance, and people need to assess and discuss behaviors that may run counter to new global leadership goals. There is also an immersion component in German business, cultural, social, and political issues. A German CEO talked to the group, as did a journalist and high-ranking government official. All this facilitated viewing the global marketplace from a European frame of reference.

The next phase of the Action Learning program called for participants to lock into a specific business project. Armed with the information, tools, and personal insights of the first phase, teams were given very real and challenging assignments. G.E., for instance, had just made an acquisition that gave them an opportunity to increase their share of the lighting market in Western Europe. Could the team think of ways G.E. might fundamentally change the rules of the lighting game? Was the market ready for a new player? Could G.E. actually change the market, and if so, how?

Confronting these questions required teams to go into the field in Europe and interview scores of customers, suppliers, and others. As they moved through Europe conducting interviews, they began to absorb everything from consumer preferences and legislative issues to the nuances of language. After team members shared their research with each other and reconvened in Brussels, they faxed their reports in. They returned to the United States and met again to prepare their final presentations.

The Action Learning program did not end, however, after the presentations to business unit heads. Feedback and reflection are critical elements in the personal transformation process. As valuable as the hands-on experiences were in Europe, they were not enough. Although many people may have changed their thinking about what it takes to be a global leader, they also needed to experience change on a deeper level. To that end, a series of follow-up meetings were held, designed as feedback and reflection vehicles.

Project teams met and engaged in an open-ended discussion about how they rated themselves as teams. Participants also received personal feedback based on their LES surveys and personal objectives. The sessions were emotionally charged but also highly structured. As a result, people were able to express their feelings and comment on behaviors in ways that were clearly related to business issues.

The Action Learning project ended with a meeting with Jack Welch. Though CEOs are not always part of the process, their participation (or the participation of other top-level executives) sends a clear message about the importance of Action Learning. In this instance, Welch met with teams and talked about their projects and how what they were doing related to the new values G.E. was attempting to instill. Welch was so impressed by the work of two of the teams that he asked them to present their recommendations to the corporate executive council, and a number of their ideas were implemented. This helped show everyone at G.E. the overlap between Action Learning and the real world of business.

Planning Global Action Learning

G.E. had a clear set of leadership issues it wanted its global Action Learning program to focus on. They had defined the strategic and business challenges facing the company and understood the qualities managers needed to acquire to meet those challenges. Unlike some organizations, they understood that globalization was not a matter of *where* they did business, but *how*. Lots of companies market their products in foreign countries. If being a global company means nothing more than exporting products, not much leadership training is needed; but if being a global company is a mindset rather than a location—as it was and is for G.E.—the values and skills required are more complex. Unlike most leadership training, Action Learning is capable of dealing with this complexity. It can help future leaders come to terms with the subtleties and ambiguities that come with a global marketplace.

Let us look at two of the most common, complex issues that organizations face. First is the issue of managing vertically and horizontally at the same time. Today's global leaders are finding themselves torn between local vertical requirements (distribution, buying and selling, measurement) and horizontal corporate ones (brand, franchise, positioning). Conflicts are inevitable, and global managers must learn how to prioritize requirements and balance demands. They will face situations that call for quick action on a local level though the corporate culture calls for consensus: Do they choose to seize an opportunity while it is there and consensus be damned? During Action Learning programs, we have heard people talk about "divided loyalties," referring to competing local and corporate accountability. Action Learning is often geared to teach people to deal with this paradoxical, ambiguous situation.

The second issue involves cross-cultural differences. Many people feel that they handle this issue well by studying a given country's language, history, and business customs. All this is fine, but it does not address the cultural differences that exist below the surface. The way an American executive feels about management, teamwork, deadlines and ethics can clash with another country's beliefs. One leader may not realize that his "damn-the-torpedoes" approach—which has won him plaudits and promotions in the United States—strikes people from another country as boorish. In fact, he almost certainly does not realize it. Our cultural biases are unconscious and so we may think we are being open-minded and flexible when we are actually being small-minded and rigid. Sometimes we have the best of intentions. I (David) once was part of a top management group that included people from France, Great Britain, and Italy. At one point the CEO asked each of us to create a rationale for global manufacturing, including recommendations for which plants might be closed in different parts of the world. When we presented our recommendations and suggested which plants might be closed and which ones should remain open, somehow, no one advocated closing a plant in their native country. Consciously or not, we were influenced by our cultural biases. We could rationalize our recommendations all we wanted—the fact remained that our biases had an impact.

Learning to Lead in the Middle of Complexity and Conflict

Most U.S. business people have some difficulty forming close relationships with people who are significantly different from themselves, are from different cultures, or have different values. This difference prevents them from letting down their defenses and opening up to a Japanese or Russian colleague, for instance; they can work with them, but they cannot establish the same bond as with another American. Yet these relationships are precisely what is necessary for effective global leadership. When dealing with complexity and uncertainty, trust and openness become critical. In a virtual world, leaders are even more dependent on teams and networks of people from different places. The best leaders will be able to work with teams composed of people from many different countries; they will be able to work as closely with them as if they all came from the same M.B.A. program or geographic region.

Creating trust is a key skill that will make strong business relationships possible, and Action Learning helps develop it. Many managers operate on the assumption that their cultural values are widely shared: "We are all Americans; we bleed IBM blue; we communicate similarly, business is business, and let's put the cards on the table." When people with strong assumptions encounter someone who does not share these assumptions, they become distrustful. This may be unconscious, but most managers in global settings will acknowledge that they can feel confused by a foreign counterpart or that they do not understand what motivates them or why they do what they do. Trust has not developed, and neither has a solid working relationship.

In Action Learning, we attempt to develop that trust. Through 360-degree feedback and other assessment devices, participants see themselves as others see them. Outward, physical challenges can quickly demonstrate the importance of trusting others to physically achieve a goal, no matter who the others are. Business projects are assigned that cannot be completed successfully unless team members drop their defenses, open their feelings and creativity, and capitalize on each other's strengths. In Global Action Learning workshops, the design incorporates conflict, ambiguity, and complexity. Leaders who emerge are those who form the relationships that allow them to function effectively in that environment.

The Process: Variations on a Theme

Organizations initiate the Action Learning process by focusing on a global leadership need that is going unmet. Sometimes it is the realization that the company's executives are ineffective when sent to manage a foreign office. Sometimes it is the less obvious but no less compelling understanding that the company's future lies in a global mindset, and that its people have not been trained to think globally. Sometimes Action Learning is built around a specific problem or opportunity—a foreign market product introduction or system redesign that provides a great opportunity for on-the-job learning.

In just about every Action Learning program with a global focus, certain elements are constant:

- A steering group is formed to oversee the Action Learning sessions; they determine the strategic objectives for the program and make sure it stays on track.

- Participants in the program are selected by the group with input from key HR processes such as talent reviews and other sources, usually with an eye for global leadership potential.

- Workshops are frequently held on-site (in the relevant foreign country) to address specific problems or opportunities in a given country or region of the world.

Beyond these common elements, Action Learning can roll out in a variety of ways, depending on the sponsoring organization's objectives. To understand the possible global variations, here is how two world class companies have used Action Learning by focusing on individual rather than team projects.

Johnson & Johnson

Johnson & Johnson recognized that their human resources executives were not consistently good business partners with global clients. Many of them concentrated on their "local" human resources responsibilities and failed to partner with other offices throughout their part of the world; they did not work well with other functions on teams and they did not take larger corporate issues into consideration in their planning. As expert as they might have been at human resources, they were not acting like business leaders.

As a result, Johnson & Johnson began Action Learning workshops for HR executives in Asia, Europe, and Latin America. Three workshops were held in these areas of the world over a sixteen-week period. During that time, the chronology of the Action Learning program was as follows:

- Participants arrived at the first workshop in Bangkok with a well thought-out change project for their business. They had been asked to come to the first workshop with this project in mind, as well as with a detailed analysis of their business and value drivers, strategic plans, and other relevant data. To provide the intellectual foundation to be a better business partner, a team-based activity called for them to explore how HR and the line could add value to Johnson & Johnson's business. Another activity forced them to confront how their own HR role was changing. Feedback about their performance from peers and colleagues segued the discussion from business to personal perspectives, and an outdoor activity helped them learn how to do "rapid team building"—a skill of critical importance if they were to become good business partners. Participants also created short vignettes that contrasted the old HR function with the new—this was done as much as a tension release from the high-pressure environment as for actual learning. Finally, the participants were given tools designed to help them collect data related to their change project—data that they would use in the second workshop.

- In this second workshop (eight weeks after the first one), participants brought back the data they had collected through interviewing, as well as an action plan for change. The goal of this second workshop was to help participants analyze their change plans and work toward implementing them in conjunction with their president. One of the unusual activities of this workshop involved team-on-team analysis of change plans—this provided multiple viewpoints on the positives and negatives of their processes.

- Participants brought the presidents of their companies to the third workshop. Between the second and third workshops, their change projects were implemented, and in the final workshop they analyzed their performance and their projects. What might they improve to be a better business partner; what were their strengths and weaknesses from a team standpoint; how did they work with other HR leaders from different countries; were they able to use new skills to deal with the complexity and conflicting interests associated with their change plan? Answering these questions in the presence of their presidents and peers made this last session emotionally intense, and it removed it from the realm of "training exercise."

Arthur Andersen

A key goal of this leading accounting firm has been to encourage their partners and expand their role from auditor to business partner. This is especially important on a global scale, where clients increasingly expect Andersen to serve them in a coordinated way around the world. Andersen is using Action Learning to help partners change how they think and act—they want their key people to become partners with CEOs, not merely accountants who proffer outstanding advice and auditing assurance.

Andersen's Action Learning program differs from Johnson & Johnson's in a number of respects. Perhaps the biggest difference is the use of coaches as part of the process. Participants have been assigned coaches who meet with them regularly for one year and work with them on task and relationship issues. The coach helps participants create a learning agenda and an action plan. Workshops are used in tandem with these coaches, where a mixture of psychological and cognitive tools are employed. Participants study the factors that influence performance and communications in different countries, and they receive feedback about their own performance and communication. Arthur Andersen wants partners to confront their current successful behavior and acquire the knowledge and tools to change that behavior and develop new skills. Making the move from thinking and acting like an auditor to thinking and acting like a global business partner is not easy. The emotional intensity of the workshops combined with the knowledge and tools offered help participants make that transition.

Conquering the World from the Inside Out

How do you rationalize an Action Learning program to achieve global objectives? Put somewhat indelicately: How do you make the argument that to become a truly global company, you need leaders who think and act in ways that are often literally and figuratively foreign?

For many organizations, globalization is defined as an external barrier challenge. Conquering new markets is like conquering new territory—if you have a good plan, a strong, well-equipped army, and sufficient boldness, you can overcome whatever resistance competitors or consumers put up. For this reason, many global strategies emphasize cognitive learning. Companies that provide global executive development arm their future global leaders with a great deal of information; they train them about how business functions in other countries; they basically tell them, "This is what works in China."

The problem is, this is not how it works. If we have learned nothing else, it is that there is no one right way. The most successful global organizations are the ones that are the most adaptable. Their leaders are able to reconcile opposites and manage effectively even in volatile business and political environments. Above all else, these successful global leaders are good at working with all sorts of people with all sorts of beliefs. They have learned to trust foreign business people who run their organizations in ways that do not conform to the Western world model. They can get past barriers of language, policy, politics, and culture and form lasting, productive relationships.

Action Learning breaks down these barriers. As the examples of G.E., Johnson & Johnson, and Arthur Andersen point out, it is possible to expand people's horizons quickly and turn them into global thinkers. Many participants have entered our programs thinking about business issues from narrow perspectives—from the perspectives of their education, their company philosophy, and their functional expertise. Action Learning forced them to confront this limited perspective and to examine how it translates into behaviors that prevent them from being business partners with people unlike themselves or from functioning effectively in unfamiliar environments.

Or let us look at it another way. One of the biggest obstacles to global leadership is a country's all-consuming culture. Leadership ideas and behaviors stem directly from culture. André Laurent, of a major European business school, conducted a well-known study that illustrates this point. For instance, he found that Japanese leaders abhor not knowing the answer to a subordinate's question. American executives, on the other hand, do not consider this to be even a minor requirement of leadership. The influence of culture is strong but not obvious and it often makes it difficult for business leaders from different countries to work together and to form strong, deep, and lasting relationships. Strong individuals in leading roles are easily frustrated with their foreign counterpart's attitudes or philosophies; they cannot understand why others cannot do business "the right" way. One's sense of control is reduced in a way that it rarely is in our own milieu.

Action Learning helps get past this attitude. It is not necessary to lecture people about the need to be open-minded, or supply case histories about why learning to function in a climate of conflict and ambiguity is beneficial. Cognitive training approaches only provide some insight. Action Learning sets up a parallel world on foreign soil, a world much like the real one except with more freedom to experiment with new behaviors and test new skills. Struggling with challenging business and personal issues, participants are pushed hard to deal with their feelings and actions. It is intense by design; 360-degree feedback is not easy to absorb. Within almost every company, some participants reacted negatively and either did not see the value of negative feedback or rationalized the validity of the source.

If there were an easier way to recreate leaders, we would endorse it. As most companies learn, however, finding people who make a quick, smooth transition from domestic to global management is difficult. The strangeness of new political systems, odd customs, nonsensical policies, elaborate social structures, and a multitude of unusual, seemingly unethical, and often incomprehensible business practices challenges even the most confident leaders.

Action Learning helps people make the transition to the demands of global teamwork and leadership. It does so not by jamming information down people's throats, but by opening their eyes to truths about themselves and to alternative paths to take.

Actions and Learnings

In setting up an Action Learning program with global intent, it is easy to fall into traps that have become standard operating procedure in many global leadership programs. To avoid these traps, the following list of do's and don'ts may prove helpful:

1. *Don't* focus the program on learning "things" about foreign cultures—the language, the business policies, the history, the geography. *Do* focus the program on experiencing what that culture is like, giving participants the chance to explore the intangibles that define how business is conducted in a given country and, most importantly, to better understand their own culture and how it shapes their view of the world.

2. *Don't* assume participants are open to new experiences and are comfortable working with people with different beliefs and values. *Do* structure sessions that allow people to talk about culture shock and to vent their prejudices and perspectives about working in foreign contexts or with those from different cultures.

3. *Don't* ignore the inherent conflict between local needs and corporate requirements. *Do* address this conflict by providing participants with projects that test how they deal with this conflict as well as feedback from coaches and other participants as to how they are dealing with it and adaptively problem solving.

4. *Don't* assemble Action Learning teams of people who are all from the same function, business unit, or country. *Do* create as diverse a team as possible.

5. *Don't* allow diverse individuals on teams to work together without confronting their biases or lack of trust in each other. *Do* provide the team with a coach who is skilled at using team-building exercises and other tools to surface the distrust and help participants work through it.

6. *Don't* hold Action Learning workshops in foreign countries and expose participants only to the same things a typical tourist would experience. *Do* have them interact with government officials, business owners, customers, academics, and the media.

7. *Don't* structure and streamline the Action Learning process to the point that all the common irritants and obstacles of working in a foreign country are removed. *Do* allow participants to face these irritants and obstacles as part of whatever business project they are working on.

6

Breaking the Boundaries
Between Functions and Business Units

Despite talk, research, and advice about the importance of working cross-functionally and across boundaries, a strong functional model still is the reality in most organizations. Re-engineering, a renewed emphasis on customer needs, and technology have certainly weakened the model, but thinking that most organizations have moved from strong silos to flexible teams or process-designed companies is a mistake.

Pledging fealty to cross-functionality is one thing, but transitioning leaders to its practice is quite another. Action Learning has the capability to help people break down the barriers between functions; it can also help leaders learn to remove the barriers between business units. Before demonstrating how this can be done, let us get a sense of the history and strength of these barriers. It is important to understand the hold functions have on people, not just intellectually, but psychologically.

Blame It on the Prussians: A Brief History of the Functional Model and the Problems Therein

It was not General Motors but a general in the Prussian army who produced the first functional model corporations have used for the past hundred years. In the 1870s, the Prussians organized their military around divisions, each with a distinct purpose. This tactic was in response to mistakes their tacticians noted were made by the Union armies during the American Civil War, which were organized around geography. This functional model has many advantages both for the military and organizations, including

- Accountability

- Control

- Coordinated disparate tasks to achieve specific goals

- Centralized authority on top to create distinct chain of command

- Predictability

In a knowledge-based, team-oriented, global world like ours, however, this functional model is as out of date as the pointy helmets the Prussian generals wore. It prevents the holistic, intuitive thinking required to deal with issues that are more complex and ambiguous than in the past. It obviates big picture perspectives, making it difficult for one functional person to understand how her work dovetails with another function to achieve a larger objective. Companies with functional structures find it hard to implement great ideas that do not fit neatly into one function's domain. These organizations also experience tremendous resistance when they try to move product ideas across divisional boundaries, especially when they try to move them quickly.

So why do companies persist in holding on to this anachronistic model? Let us look at the five most compelling reasons:

1. *The organizational socialization process.* Most top managers were raised in a functional hierarchy. They were promoted because of how well they did within their function. They viewed those in other functions with indifference and sometimes distrust. Psychologically, they feel most comfortable

working with others like themselves; they also prefer this structure to others because they know it so well. From the standpoint of self-interest, they have benefited from it. As soon as one of their own reaches a position of prominence, he brings others in his function up the ladder. This fraternal culture is very difficult to transcend, no matter what the realities of the marketplace dictate.

2. *Size*. Some companies have become large and unwieldy so the functional structure seems to be the only one that will work. It at least gives management the illusion that things are under control, tasks will get done, and people will be held accountable. Of course, in this quest for control, the needs of the customer are often lost—we forget that customers do not look at things from a functional perspective, and we cannot expect customers to adapt to an organization in order to be served.

3. *The lean mentality*. When organizations run in the lean stretch mode—as more and more are doing—it is very difficult to develop people cross-functionally. Moving people from function to function requires an investment in time and money that most companies simply cannot afford to make.

4. *It is intimidating*. Perhaps this is a subset of reason 1, but it is so significant that we feel it deserves its own number. Cross-functional structures require giving up a certain amount of control, decreasing accountability, and thinking about business problems from new and unfamiliar perspectives. It is human nature to be scared of the unknown, and cross-functionality challenges a lot of executives because it increases complexity and decreases authority.

5. *Antipathy between functions*. This particular reason is analogous to countries with years of distrust between them. Even though Russia and the United States now seek to cooperate, the governments still harbor a good deal of suspicion of each other. The conflicts inherent between functions are legend.

Design people seem to always look for the most "elegant" solutions whereas manufacturing just wants to meet the needs of customers. Finance people want to control costs but marketing people say, "Let's grow the business and costs be damned." This tension is inherent and typically healthy—unless it develops into distrust and suspicion.

Why Cross-Functional Efforts Fail

Even when organizations overcome all the reasons to keep functional systems in place and attempt to reduce the boundaries, they still run into problems. To segue from functional to cross-functional structures requires a powerful tool, and the tools many companies are using are ineffective.

One of the biggest problems is that many companies are all talk but no action learning; they talk about the need to work cross-functionally but lack any process to make that talk a part of the leadership personality. The cross-functional re-creation of leaders is not just cognitive, it is also psychological. Though organizations may be awash in cross-functional teams, the leadership may still work from a hardcore functional platform. Consider the CEO of a food company, a CEO who had only a strong marketing background. As much as he endorsed the cross-functional teams formed by his company, he spent 70 percent of his time on marketing issues. To him, this was what had the greatest impact on the company's core business. As a result, he spent little time focusing on significant manufacturing and operations problems—problems that were a direct result of manufacturing and operations people's attempts to follow the CEO's marketing lead. The FDA came down hard on the company and threatened them with huge penalties. With a little cross-functional thinking on the CEO's part, about $100 million in rework could have been avoided.

The other major problem is that cross-functional teams and cross-functional leaders have the authority but not the power to implement decisions. In other words, their empowerment is in name only. Organizations fear stepping on political toes by taking power away from functional department heads and spreading it across functions. We have seen many of these teams denied approval for their cross-functional decisions or their freedom to make those decisions severely limited when a team member reports back to her functional boss. When top management is not fully supportive and involved in the cross-functional system, disputes, indecision, and even sabotage result.

As we shall see, Action Learning ensures the support and involvement of management and re-creates leaders intellectually and psychologically.

Fresh Frames of Reference

Action Learning forces people to look at business issues differently. Perhaps that is putting it too mildly. What it really does is expose participants to an array of new people and ideas and demand that they confront their own parochial views of the business. It does this by

- *Varying the normal composition of teams.* Action Learning does not just mean creating a cross-functional team (though the juxtaposition of different functions is important). It may involve putting together people from different levels of the organization—levels that do not ordinarily mix. The mixture may be geographical— a team that is global in composition, for instance—or it may be drawn from separate business units that rarely if ever interact. The key is to expose team members to new and sometimes conflicting points of view.

- *Setting up interactions with "outsiders."* These outsiders can include customers, government officials, academics, community leaders, and others. The idea is to give people a sense of how others view not only the business, but issues that affect the business. For instance, Action Learning teams at General Electric Information Systems fanned out across Europe interviewing customers. For many team members, this was a first. Many of them were high-tech and financial people who had precious little customer contact. After the intensive interviewing, one team member said, "I'll never bitch about those marketing people again."

- *Working on tasks outside of one's function.* The rule-of-thumb at GE was that every Action Learning team member had to work on a project outside his or her functional area. You can imagine how this might befuddle some people. Someone who has spent twenty years in human resources suddenly has to deal with a thorny financial problem, or an objective-driven sales person has to explore long-term strategy. It's a disorienting experience to grapple with unfamiliar issues, which is precisely the point.

- *Participating in high-level strategy-making.* Action Learning can offer participants the chance to experience the power of true leaders. Many companies we have worked for—Ameritech, Shell Oil, and Johnson & Johnson are three that immediately come to mind—specifically designed Action Learning programs that gave participants the chance to shape strategy. Many of the participants had not reached a level of responsibility where they had done strategic planning before, at least not in a meaningful way. Many Action Learning participants must rise to this new level of responsibility and perspective. Given the opportunity to lead the company in a given direction, they transcend functional biases and prejudices toward other functions and business units. They begin to see the need to lead holistically rather than from a narrow base.

- *Confronting "dys-functional" behaviors.* People are not always aware of their functional prejudices. They do not always realize how much they resent and misunderstand people from another business unit. Within an Action Learning format, there are a number of opportunities to surface and confront these feelings. Outdoor, physical experiences and other bonding group activities help participants learn to trust and work with fellow employees. As part of this process, they discover that individuals are not as marginal or difficult as their functional roles might have suggested.

Some team exercises also help surface these feelings. One effective Action Learning method we frequently use that has been available for many years is called "Win as Much as You Can," a game of paradox in which teams are divided into competing groups and asked to choose the letters X or Y. The teams are told that the greatest potential winning comes from choosing X, but that potential is realized only if everyone else chooses Y; that losses come if everyone chooses X; that small but consistent winnings come when everyone chooses Y. This exercise provokes intense debate, as teams struggle to come to grips with the "Us-Them" paradox. Should a team trust other teams and choose Y so that everyone wins on a small scale? Should they abandon other teams and try to win as much as they can by choosing X? As the debate rages, team members frequently say things about others like, "He is a marketing guy, and they always put themselves first, so we can count on him choosing X," or "She is part of human resources, and they're soft—I know her team will choose Y." Facilitators use these feelings to get at deeper biases, misconceptions, and ultimately issues of trust.

The stress and feedback that are part of every Action Learning event also allow participants to confront these issues. Whatever the goal of an event, the structure dictates that team members will be accountable for the ideas they produce, that they will be placed under significant deadline and emotional pressure, that they will present their ideas to senior management, and that they will receive feedback about their ideas and behaviors from other team members and management throughout the process. In the heat of the moment, participants are likely to reveal feelings about other functions and business units that they normally keep under wraps (either consciously to avoid offending or unconsciously). We have found that when people bring their feelings out in the open and talk them through, they can often move past them.

For people to be re-created into leaders who think and act in boundaryless ways, they must move past years of assumptions and misunderstandings. Although it does not always happen overnight, the tools and techniques discussed here greatly accelerate the process. The ultimate goal is in the ideas and recommendations that come out of Action Learning workshops. Though people might enter these events with functional mindsets, they emerge as holistic thinkers and re-created leaders. Let us look at a few examples of these ideas and recommendations.

Seeing Forward, Not Backward

Citibank is divided into five business units, two of which are the Global Relationship Bank (focusing on developed markets) and the Emerging Markets group (focusing on developing markets). An Action Learning program was held, and a team was asked to determine how traders from both businesses might improve their use of Citibank resources to serve customers better.

This was not a new issue. Getting different groups within Citibank to maximize limited resources to save money and serve customers more effectively had long been an overarching goal. Certainly, people gave lip service to cooperating more with other units, sacrificing for the common good of the company and sharing resources, but when push came to shove, everyone would dig in and fight for their turf.

The Action Learning program, however, brought a lot of issues into the open. It became clear that there were tensions and some distrust between the Global Relationship and Emerging Markets groups. By acknowledging this fact, expressing fears and concerns, hearing what the "other person" had to say all within the Action Learning crucible, this tension and distrust dissolved.

The recommendation that evolved from the Action Learning event would never have been produced under other circumstances. It required an openness and free exchange of information between people from the two business units that simply was impossible before. What emerged was the conclusion that highly compensated executives from both business groups were being poorly deployed; that an amazing 70 percent of transactions in both units did not require the participation of these executives; and that other personnel or electronic transactions could provide the same level of service in these transactions. The team's recommendation was implemented, and it helped save top people from both business units for the big, complex transactions where their skills were especially valuable.

Besides the Global Relationship Bank and Emerging Markets, Citibank has three other business units: Credit Cards, Private Bank (for affluent, individual customers), and Citibanking (consumer branch banking). One of Citibank's concerns is improving performance in the "white spaces" between the five business units. Team Challenge was the name for a series of Action Learning events designed to foster that improvement. During the first Team Challenge program, teams focused on potential synergies between the units—synergies that could only be realized if barriers between the units were broken down. For example, Cards and Citibanking frequently share the same customers, but if a customer loses her purse, she has to call one number to report her credit card lost and another for checking. Functions are duplicated, customers are peeved, and opportunities for cross-selling are lost.

Action Learning helped open participants' eyes to these problems and the concomitant opportunities. It dissolved barriers that had been years in the making. Suddenly, people were not jealously guarding their business unit turf; they were able to see ideas for profit and growth that had been invisible before.

To help you see what Action Learning participants saw, consider this idea that emerged from one of the events. The team recommended establishing a single 800 number for both Credit Cards and Citibanking customers, supported by a sophisticated computer system. The idea was that on the front end, callers would be routed by computer to the Citibank representative who best met their needs—this computerized front end would not only save customers time, it would save Citibank money and increase efficiency. Their recommendation also had an ingenious back-end concept. When a caller is directed to a Credit Card representative, that representative may learn that the caller has just moved from one part of the country to another part. The recommended new computer/phone system would prompt the representative to ask whether the customer was interested in mortgage information and, if so, make it easy to transfer the caller to a representative from the other business unit.

Without Action Learning, it would have been difficult for even a cross-functional team to come up with this idea. Presenting business unit managers with white area customers is like giving two small children a toy and asking them to share: Fights often break out. At Citibank, managers were able to transcend this mindset and capitalize on the holistic thinking of re-created leaders.

How One Functional Manager Was Re-Created

When we talk about how future leaders can shed their functional or business unit baggage, we are often greeted with skepticism. Though people may accept the notion of re-creating leaders in other ways, this one often engenders doubts. We are all aware of how indoctrinated people become—how years of working only with one type of person can produce ingrained biases and misconceptions. Many of us have witnessed the failure of cross-functional teams to reduce these biases and misconceptions. Though cross-functional teams do bring different functions together, they lack the power to transform. They are typically cognitive experiences, missing the emotional component necessary to catalyze changes in the way people feel about other functions (while there can be an emotional component in cross-functional teams, it usually occurs by chance and not as a planned part of the process).

Action Learning has both cognitive and emotional components. To show you how they work in concert, let's look at a real individual, Brian, and his experience with Action Learning.

Brian is an Ameritech financial executive; he has worked in the financial area since receiving his M.B.A. seventeen years ago. As part of an Action Learning program, he was placed on a team of people who represented purchasing, the Network, customer service, marketing, and human resources. They were asked to examine key external regulatory issues facing Ameritech and to recommend a course of action. One of the ideas that quickly emerged and gained the team's favor involved trading local market dominance for long-distance market opportunities. Brian, however, was very resistant to this concept at first. Falling back on his financial background, he immediately shifted into cost analysis of the issue and saw the downside potential. Brian led the debate against developing this idea.

The debate and discussion were helpful to Brian in the sense that it was his first real opportunity for extended dialogue and to build trust with people from other functions. He gained some insight into their concerns and experiences, but he still stuck to his financial guns. His gut told him that the tradeoff was too risky and even dangerous to the business.

As part of the Action Learning process, 360-degree feedback provided participants with insights about everything from their ideas to their team behaviors. Although Brian received some compliments about his financial acumen, he also received some criticism for his "pigheadedness when it comes to listening to what others have to say." Or as another team member put it: "Brian, you're a good guy and a smart guy, but when someone suggests an idea, you usually look at it for what will go wrong rather than what can go right."

This shook Brian a bit, but he did not change his mind. He figured that *their problem* was their non-financial backgrounds; they did not know what he knew about how many things could go wrong.

Still, the team had to arrive at consensus on a recommendation soon. Brian and everyone else was conscious that this was not just another "learning experience"; they were all expected to perform and careers could be affected by their performance. In fact, one requirement was that the team would rate every member on his or her performance—that anyone who was not performing up to expectations would know it. This "external" motivation put a certain amount of pressure on Brian. But he also put pressure on himself. He recognized that being selected for an Action Learning program was inherent recognition, and he wanted to do well. He also was energized by the diverse people on his team, people he found to be smart and savvy.

Each time they met, he came to know his team members a bit better. The debate and feedback made him examine his own position. The research and benchmarking the team did exposed Brian to new data that challenged his position. Brian also began to react differently to the criticism he was receiving. At first, he had been defensive. Now, he felt badly that he was letting the team down in some way. It was a strange feeling. Here's what Brian said about it: "I've always identified with finance; I trusted finance people more than I trust anyone else in Ameritech. But over time, working with my Breakthrough Leadership (Action Learning) team, I began to identify with them. It was like *The Dirty Dozen*, where all these guys are thrown together to accomplish an important mission. The pressure creates a bond among the team. It was almost unconscious, the

way I switched my emotional connection from the finance department to the team. It was powerful."

Brian had not become brainwashed or swayed by the majority
opinion. He started to think at a higher level, less inhibited by his
functional biases.

Actions and Learnings

Sometimes companies have difficulty recognizing the impact of silos
and other boundaries on the thought processes of their emerging
leaders. To determine whether this is an issue in your organization,
answer the following questions. The more "yes" answers you have,
the more likely it is that your people are afflicted by this issue.

1. Did the majority of people in top management come up through
   only one or two functions?

2. When people achieve general management roles in your organization, do they tend to favor people in their previous functions
   with key assignments and promotions?

3. Do most of the top executives in your organization share the
   same functional expertise as your CEO?

4. Are you a large organization where management has had a history
   of exerting control through a hierarchical reporting relationship?

5. Is it unusual for your company to move fast-trackers from function to function in order to develop them (as opposed to moving
   them up the functional ladder)?

6. Is there a reluctance to invest money or time in any cross-
   functional or cross-business development (especially if you are
   currently operating in a lean mode)?

7. Would functional heads in your company resist giving up real
   decision-making power authority in order to invest it in cross-
   function or cross-business unit teams?

8. Are there historical feuds between certain functions in your company?

If you find yourself answering "yes" to many of these questions, you are well aware that functional boundaries can, in fact, be brick walls. If this is the case, an Action Learning process may include a number of elements that seem odd or controversial. Here is a list of elements we recommend using to re-create boundaryless leaders:

1. *Find the combustible mix of Action Learning participants given the problems and prejudices of your organization.* If there is animosity between marketing and finance, be sure to include members of both groups on a team. If two business units have always operated at a certain remove from each other, include members from each.

2. *Select participants based on unfamiliarity with each other.* Not just animosity between functions and business units causes problems, but a lack of contact. Create an unusual mix, even if you have people working together who seem ill-matched (a dynamic, aggressive sales manager and a quiet, conservative accountant, for instance).

3. *Choose a sufficiently challenging business project that requires people to work together to produce a solid recommendation (rather than relying on individual, functional expertise for a solution).* In other words, force people to stretch; give them a task that demands they draw upon each other's different talents and knowledge.

4. *Reinforce the previous point by having them work together on a team-building exercise.* A risk-taking outdoor activity, an unfamiliar task such as cooking or music, or the exercise described earlier in the chapter are good examples of team-building metaphors.

5. *Surface biases, myths, and misconceptions about other functions or business units through discussion, feedback, and coaching*

and give participants time to reflect on what they are learning.
Point out biases and prejudices directly and elevate conflicts to
an open level for resolution. As uncomfortable that it might be to
tell a participant that she harbors certain prejudices, it is critical.
Giving that participant time to think about her attitudes and the
feedback she has received is just as important.

7

Reconceptualizing the Business

One of the most challenging tasks for emerging leaders is to think about the business in new ways. It is difficult for veteran telephone or utility executives to adjust to life after deregulation, or for health care company advertising executives to adjust to a cost-driven industry. It has required a major shift in virtually every area of strategy and policy. In organization after organization, shifts of this magnitude are taking place. In the past, leaders were required to shift their thinking, but often over the course of an entire career, not in eighteen months. Reconceptualization, however, requires a sea change in perspective, often demanding a 180-degree swing in attitudes and behaviors and aborting both learned experience and historical success patterns. Reconceptualization is very much a part of this new business era, and most companies have little experience—beyond providing training in the classroom about new ideas, information, and methods—in helping their leaders make the transition from historical ways of doing business to new and unfamiliar ways.

Re-creating leaders who can reconceptualize a business is an equally difficult task. When you ask leaders to think about their business in a new way, you are also (implicitly) asking them to take on a changed role in a changed business. They may be able to conceive of transforming a company from, for example, a centralized to a decentralized structure, or a country structure to a global one, but

they cannot conceive of how they would actually function effectively without a team of subordinates to do what is needed.

If all this were not tough enough, reconceptualization is continuous. In other words, the skill is not to reconceive the business
once; it is the capacity continually to reinvent it.

Given the difficulty of acquiring this skill, the question becomes:
Is it worth the effort? Even if you accept that Action Learning can
facilitate the ability to reconceptualize, you may wonder whether this
is one skill re-created leaders can do without. After all, is reconceptualization not the job of the CEO or at least the top team? Is there
not a precedent for a few visionary leaders at the senior levels reframing the business and leading the way? Are not books written about
famous individuals who single-handedly transformed their company?

The One Versus the Many

In the old business paradigm, it was assumed that reframing the
business was the top team's role. The prevalent idea was that the
person at the top was in the best position to change the company's
course, because he or she could naturally see the most. Even in the
new business paradigm, the notion persists that CEOs are the
visionary heroes who blaze paths into new markets and technologies, carrying others along. The era of the CEO as company hero
has prevailed for a decade, and many successful transformations fea-
ture the CEO as a hero: Sam Walton with his low-cost, no-frills
warehouse shopping; Jack Welch turning G.E. into a customer-
focused, global company; Al Dunlop restructuring Scott paper and
Sunbeam; Bill Gates resisting the Internet and then embracing it.

These and other well-known CEOs have received the majority
of the credit for moving their companies in successful new directions. Though they deserve credit, their success could not have been
achieved without other reconceptualizers (and heros) at all levels
of the business leadership. We know that because we have run
Action Learning events in many of these companies and have

observed the contributions of other people. Let us look at some of the advantages of having many reconceptualizers at all levels:

- *Reduces resistance to change.* People do not necessarily resist change; they do resist change being done to them. The CEO may develop a great new strategy for the business or the future, but if he thrusts it upon employees, they may resist though perhaps indirectly. If, however, certain key employees are included in the change-making process, they are more likely to buy into it and convince their subordinates to buy in. Action Learning opens up the process, helping a cross-section of future leaders to participate in reconceptualizing the business. The more people possess this skill, the less resistance there will be to major change initiatives.

- *Increases the odds of making the right bet on the next technological wave.* This is true for many industries, but especially knowledge-based service industries such as health, software, law, and consulting. Teams of people with direct access to the decision makers must be looking forward, searching for the next technological wave, and planning how to turn the company into that wave when it comes into view. One person cannot do this alone or at least do it as effectively. Groups of reconceptualizers are needed not only to spot the next technology, but to analyze its impact and determine how best to capitalize on it.

- *Confers psychological edge.* Reframing your view of the business is challenging. When even thinking about the dramatic changes that might be necessary both in a job and in a business, the tendency is to become tentative: "Maybe we should wait and see what develops before doing anything" is a common reaction. A company filled with skilled reconceptualizers is psychologically equipped to act decisively while competitors debate their options. They have the sense that they can face the future, no matter how much it varies from the norm. Action Learning helps participants become comfortable with reshaping strategy and rethinking assumptions. It confers the psychological edge of companies such as Microsoft, Nike, and Intel, companies that always seem to be one step ahead of the game and able to absorb any shocks to their systems. In these companies, we've learned from experience that many people are tasked with the job of reconceptualizing.

- *Brings fresh ideas, perspectives, and possibilities into the process.* When a few key leaders are the only ones rethinking the business, the rethinking grows stale. Top executives often share the same sensibilities, the same experiences, beliefs, and interests. It is a form of intellectual incest. Inviting other employees to rethink business norms democratizes the process; it creates a dialogue between individuals and the organization. Subversive, iconoclastic, and startling ideas are most likely to originate below the top layer of management. Those close to the action of customers and unbound by standard strategic thinking because they are new, young, or just "difficult" find it easiest to suggest something new and different. They are also more likely to be brutally honest about what the future holds, and often what the present is lacking. One of the great things about Action Learning is that it encourages honesty at the expense of politics. It gives numerous people the opportunity to say the company will suffer if it continues on its present path; and it gives them a structural environment with a relative freedom to suggest ways to avoid that possibility.

Given the advantages of reconceptualizing by the many, let us look at three Action Learning programs in which this was a primary goal.

Challenging Cherished Beliefs

Most people who are selected to participate in Action Learning programs have already developed strong beliefs about their businesses. They have been indoctrinated in M.B.A. programs, standard executive programs, and during the course of bureaucratic survival in everything from performance reviews to report-based structures. Shaking these beliefs requires shaking people up. Action Learning shakes people up in all sorts of ways.

At Electronic Data Systems (EDS), program participants were shaken to the core—or at least to their core competencies. In 1992, EDS was a systems developer for large clients such as General Motors. Since EDS's founding by Ross Perot thirty years before, it had grown steadily and profitably. Yet its chairman, Les Aberthal, saw slower growth and increased competition ahead, and he responded with a series of Action Learning workshops that brought together 120 key leaders. Their assignment was to examine the business and its future. Most participants began the program skeptically; they viewed the workshops as "an academic exercise" and nothing more. That view crumbled incrementally; each piece of knowledge and personal experience accumulated to the point that participants could not help but test their assumptions. At the beginning of the program, participants were asked to examine a list of Fortune 500 companies from twenty years ago; they learned that the majority of companies on that list no longer existed (because of acquisitions, mergers, or bankruptcies). Management shared EDS revenue projections that awakened middle managers and challenged them to think of how those projections might become more optimistic. Participants went through a series of programs that asked them to examine the company from a customer's perspective, seeing the future from the "bottom up" rather than the "top down." By the end of the sessions, many participants were advocating a new direction for the company, one that entailed marketing the power of information to meet both business and societal challenges.

EDS's Action Learning program was motivated by a general concern about future strategy. Johnson & Johnson, on the other hand, had very specific concerns. They wanted their key managers to reconceptualize the way they approached one of their growing businesses— Endosurgery, a worldwide medical products business whose customers are surgeons and hospitals. Johnson & Johnson recognized that their market was rapidly evolving: Single customers were being replaced by HMOs; their customers wanted knowledge (how to use Endosurgery products) as much as the products themselves; the line between customer and supplier was blurring as opportunities for product-development partnerships arose.

The Action Learning workshops in Europe brought a diverse group of managers together, including many people who had nothing to do with the Endosurgery business. Although many of the Action Learning tools and techniques were similar to those used by EDS, another element was crucial to Johnson & Johnson: They wanted their people to develop a sense of mission to find "the next big thing." Having them rethink their approach to customers was not enough. In another few years, they would need to reconceptualize once again. Johnson & Johnson hoped that their emerging leaders would be passionate about seeking the next wave that might affect the business. When their leaders found that wave, the company hoped that they would defend it, lobbying for changes in an entrepreneurial, evangelical manner. Johnson & Johnson wanted to replace the old skill of being able to execute a strategy in a disciplined manner with the new skill of reconceptualizing with fire and creativity.

Just mention the name, Ameritech, and the need to reconceptualize the business becomes obvious. Ameritech's future depended on immediate and serious rethinking of the company's role. As

Ameritech prepared to move from the regulated environment, management saw the enormous shift people needed to make. Imagine having worked for years in a competition-free marketplace, where returns on assets could be handled just by raising prices, where the culture insisted that things be done methodically and expensively. As a result of this climate, competitive energy was directed inward—toward other departments, individuals, or perceived threats.

Ameritech recognized that lectures, classes, and manuals were insufficient to meet the challenge of reconceptualization. To get Ameritech's change agents to develop their best ideas quickly for both strategy and culture, a more dynamic, profound process was needed. They wanted their people to be able to change reward systems, reengineer jobs, and redesign the entire sales process. That is why Action Learning became an integral component of Ameritech's reconceptualization.

Reconceptualizing Catalysts

We have touched on some of the ways Action Learning helps people see the business world anew, now let us identify the major methodologies:

- *Introducing thought-provoking, status quo–challenging information.* The right data presented or discovered in the right way can instigate the reassessment. In Action Learning programs, the introduction of provocative data is one of the first and most important activities. It can be done many different ways—everything from participants interviewing customers, government officials, and other experts, to learning directly from a prominent academic or theorist, and first-hand benchmarking experiences in other industries. Action Learning programs for General Electric, Johnson & Johnson, and the University of Michigan Global Leadership program have all been very ambitious in terms of the scope of data sought. In each program, participants have been dispatched throughout targeted countries, interviewing a variety of people in search of new information. By taking them out of familiar surroundings and throwing them into the marketplace, their data-gathering becomes a much more powerful experience. When they hear a customer tell them that, contrary to expectations, their revolutionary product is not so revolutionary after all, it makes an impact.

- *Creating a parallel world of transformational learning.* Action Learning produces a controlled environment that encourages risk-taking and introspection, activities that cause us to change the way we think. It is a hybrid world where teams pursue real business goals but are given the freedom to explore new information and ideas, to participate in tasks and exercises, and to give and receive feedback. The synergy between the real and the theoretical, between business and personal issues, makes reconceptualization possible. Many executives tell us that they have said and done things in Action Learning that they never would have said and done in their work environments. People are encouraged to try out new ideas, to express fears about their performance, to criticize business strategy openly. In the day-to-day reality of work, finding the time and emotional space necessary to discover a new perspective or overcome fears of reprisal is tough. In most training formats or retreats, the approach is often too theoretical or based on cases to make people seriously reexamine their views. Action Learning yields a third type of temporary system—one where people naturally reframe and rethink issues.

- *Confronting people with their behaviors and beliefs.* Most work environments do not encourage introspection. A component of every Action Learning program provides participants the opportunity to reflect. After receiving feedback about their ideas and performance from team members, people are motivated to reflect on what they believe and how they have behaved. When they consistently hear from team members that they are stubborn and resistant to change, even the toughest managers can be taken aback. They pause and think long and hard because these are their peers, and this is their company—they cannot "return home" and simply disregard the feedback. In these moments, reconceptualization can occur. Participants are vulnerable and open to new ideas. This is where they develop the capacity to relinquish a cherished and confirmed view of the culture or the marketplace and entertain new concepts.

- *Building a theory of the case.* People need a business reason to challenge their own leadership assumptions. It is not enough that they are emotionally open to the idea; they need to be pushed by cognitive analysis of problems and opportunities. In an Action Learning process, there is a great deal of data-gathering and analysis with an eye toward explaining why: Why aren't we growing; why are customers defecting; why are new competitors entering our core markets; why haven't we pursued a new technology; what is our future? A theory of the case provides a rationale for taking the next step; it makes the incomprehensible understandable and gives people a platform to come up with new ideas, solutions, and approaches. Once you understand why something has happened—or at least, once you have created a theory to explain it—you can use that knowledge to shape a vision of the future. Each leader must develop his or her own theory of the case in order to influence other people and the business.

- *Providing an environment in which a vision can emerge.* The words people use often to describe Action Learning are "open" and "safe." A problem with encouraging leaders to reconceptualize is that it is "dangerous." People are reluctant to float radical ideas for fear they will be called stupid or considered subversive. Action Learning can create an atmosphere in which the only people who are considered stupid are those who do not ask radical questions. The vision that emerges is a result of the Action Learning gestalt, the way in which participants are encouraged to explore all sorts of paths and possibilities. For instance, the Action Learning recommendations at Shell Oil gave birth to a new shared services unit (which evolved from the creation of a new governance model and decentralized business units). Sharing services in any company raises all sorts of difficult issues, from loyalty (what if a business unit decided it wanted to go outside the company for services?) to the impact on fixed costs, and Shell was no exception. "What if" questions proliferated, and the Action Learning participants conceived of a future in which a shared services unit became reality. They could never have done this as openly as in an Action Learning process in which they were encouraged to explore cost-saving scenarios—there would have been too many objections and political toes stepped on. Action Learning teams are political free zones; no one is allowed to pull rank; everyone is encouraged to be provocative and innovative in their thinking.

Diary of a Reconceptualized Manager

We would like to share with you excerpts from the journal of a General Electric manager who went through an Action Learning program in 1989. Though we have cleaned up the writing and edited for length, these journal entries provide a mind's eye view of a manager learning to reframe his thoughts about the global marketplace and his company's role in it.

By way of background, you should know that the impetus behind this Action Learning event was G.E.'s determination to globalize the company. Jack Welch was pushing hard in this direction, and he asked Paolo Fresco, senior vice president of G.E. International, to spearhead the effort. Paolo, in turn, decided to use Action Learning teams to analyze the global situation. Specifically, he created six teams and assigned two to each of three key countries—China, the Soviet Union, and India. Their assignment was to evaluate the viability of G.E. doing business in the given country, and if it was viable, determining the type of business that made sense. People chosen for teams were aware that selection meant they were being considered for leadership positions within G.E. (general manager positions). The Action Learning event lasted approximately five weeks, and participants spent part of that time in their assigned countries.

Our journal-writer, Steven, a hypothetical manager, worked in a middle management position in a G.E. manufacturing business. Steven was chosen because he was being groomed to take over a large business unit, and the position would entail a significant amount of global work, especially in Asia. Steven was picked for the team assigned to India. Here are excerpts from his journal over the five-week period (the first entry was made a few days before the Action Learning program began):

> Greg (Steven's boss) told me that the fact I was selected
> for this program means I'm being considered for advance-
> ment, which is great, but I can't say I'm overjoyed at the

prospect of going to India. I'm not real optimistic about spotting business opportunities in a country where there's so much poverty. Still, Greg explained to me that globalization is extremely important to management, and it's in my best interests to start broadening myself in this area, since most of my travel abroad for work has been limited. I can't say I really understand how business works anywhere but in North America. Of course, it's hard to believe that there's that much difference when you get past the language and cultural issues.

The following is from the first week of the program, spent at G.E.'s Crotonville, New York training facility:

I just finished the first day, and it was quite an experience. Everything today was devoted to team building. I was placed on a team with five other people who will be going to India, and we rafted the Hudson, talked about the team process and leadership, established norms for making decisions and communicating within the team. I'm a bit overwhelmed by everything, but it's also neat to see the way the team is taking shape.

The second day:

This was my first experience with 360-degree feedback, which I've heard about from other people who have gone through Action Learning. I guess I wasn't prepared for it; I'm still a little shaken. I assumed that we were going to receive feedback about our business strengths and weaknesses. I found out that some of the feedback can get kind of personal. Though I received some compliments, I also was told that I don't communicate as clearly as I might, and sometimes I give the impression that I'm not really listening. It wasn't that the criticism was harsh or mean-spirited. It was just unexpected. Everyone had something they needed to work on, so it wasn't as if I was singled out. The way we left the discussion was that the team would observe each member and continue to give him or her feedback on how they were doing in their weak areas.

The entry from the end of the week at Crotonville:

I guess the way I'd describe this week is a kind of boot camp for the mind. Not that a lot of it hasn't been enjoyable. It's just that there have been so many things going on, I feel like I'm really being pushed to perform. One day was devoted to learning about India, which was a pretty amazing experience, given how much information they threw at us. Another day Senator Bill Bradley stopped by to talk to us about his experiences in the Soviet Union. Then Jack Welch came by and told us how important our assignment was, how much he was counting on us, and that he was looking forward to receiving our input. I suppose you could say that I feel like I'm under some pressure. But I also like the challenge of it, the chance to test myself.

After the first few days in India:

My first impression was that this is a country of contrasts. You see cows wandering through the street, but the hotel is as modern as any in the United States. New Delhi is a fascinating place and we've had a chance to experience some of it. . . . [Steven provides a fairly long description of his reactions to the culture.] You would not believe the poverty. The bureaucracy, too, is a problem; it took forever to get all the functionaries at the airport to check our papers. I can just imagine all the red tape if we tried to introduce a product.

The briefings we've received, though, make me understand why G.E. is interested in this market. We've heard from Indian academics and government officials, G.E. people who are working here, joint venture companies who have told us of their experiences. It's clear that some organizations have done well, though I'm still not quite sure how G.E. can duplicate their success.

We've talked about all these issues as a team, and that's probably been the best of the experience so far. In the past, the teams I've worked on have been composed almost exclusively of engineers like myself. Everyone on our team has a different background. One of the guys is a Japanese executive from G.E.'s Power Systems group; another is from Belgium, a manager with G.E. Plastics. Their views and experiences are so different from mine. It makes me realize how diverse a company G.E. really is.

Entry made after a series of data-gathering interviews in Calcutta and Bombay:

We've been conducting interviews in mini-teams of two for the last week with people at Indian factories, government officials, and businesses from other countries who have established offices here. It's been a whirlwind of activity. Literally. We flew through a sandstorm to get to one interview.

I also learned a lot when I struck up a friendship with an Indian engineer. He runs a plant that's in the middle of nowhere, but to my surprise, it's a joint venture with Du Pont. He invited me to his house to have dinner with his family, and he got me excited about the business possibilities. He admitted there was a lot of poverty, but he also insisted that there's a sizable middle class (100 million people!). I started to argue with him about the business potential, but I caught myself. My team has been working with me on developing my listening skills, so I shut up and listened. He made a pretty convincing case, I have to admit, but I still don't know if India is right for G.E.

I've now conducted a lot more interviews, and I've been impressed by the intelligence and business savvy of many of the Indian executives. Perhaps more than anything else, though, I'm hearing a simple refrain: The demand for products and services isn't being met by the supply. The need for quality isn't being met, and a large percentage of the people I talk with know the G.E. name and recognize the quality attached to it.

Entry made after presentation to management:

We've just finished delivering our recommendation to Paolo Fresco and his staff in London. The team meetings that preceded all this were the most intense of my life. The politeness that we all showed each other at first disappeared at times as we presented the data from our interviews and argued our positions. Part of this is that we all felt like we were under a great deal of pressure to come up with the right recommendation. But there was also something else. We all wanted to share our conclusions and present them as convincingly as we could. I think all of us felt close to each other and comfortable enough to be extremely honest and open. One guy said he thought I was overreacting to earlier criticism and was listening too much and speaking too little!

In any case, we eventually reached what I like to think of as a hard-fought consensus. We agreed to recommend that G.E. enter the Indian market. I was more than a little surprised that I was instrumental in getting the team to agree on this recommendation, since I was so skeptical at first. But I think my skepticism was a result of a lot of things—my narrow band of experience, my tendency to form strong first impressions and not listen to anyone who might threaten that strong belief. Now, I'd feel confident if G.E. asked me to manage a group that was trying to do business in India; I really think I could handle it.

In fact, I feel that I could handle a lot of things better. There's that old saying about how travel is a broadening experience. I'm not sure if it's just travel, but the chance to experience ideas and situations you've never experienced before.

Adding a Hundred Stevens to Your Company Every Year

Action Learning programs have a cumulative impact, especially at organizations like G.E. and Johnson & Johnson that use the process regularly. The reconceptualizing capacity expands exponentially. Steven will spread his insights to people he works with, informally encouraging subordinates and peers to think about their parts of the business in new ways. As a result, G.E. has built new organizational capability to reconceptualize at the drop of a hat (or a drop in market share). Right now, leaders at G.E. are still busy refocusing their core businesses, exploring ways to move from a manufacturing to a services base for the next decade. Considering that Jack Welch's commitment to Action Learning is continuous, reconceptualization will be a way of business.

Actions and Learnings

An organization's capability to reconceptualize and build leadership strengths at all levels is not acquired overnight. When reconceptualization or transformation is a key goal of Action Learning, we face a difficult challenge. We know participants have been a part of a strong culture and equally strong definition for years, and to move them to reframe and refocus is not accomplished quickly.

Earlier in the chapter, we discussed five techniques that we found useful to achieve reconceptualization goals. We would like to share with you some tips and tools that will make these techniques that much more effective.

Introducing thought-provoking, status quo–challenging information.

- Provoke. We have helped companies expose Action Learning participants to realistic doomsday scenarios, to projections of decline, to the specter of potential shareholder lawsuits. This exposure provokes people into a new frame of reference, so the data must pack a punch.

- Invite people "inside." Participants become serious when they are privy to confidential information (sales projections, industry estimates, etc.). By allowing them to absorb an extremely confidential study or see financial projections, companies impress upon them the seriousness of the subject and the seriousness of their own role.

- Reinforce the data. If an Action Learning team is exposed to provocative information, it may have an impact, but it will be far less than if they receive the same information in a variety of ways. Mixing the written reports and participant interviews with expert views on a given subject enables participants to realize that they need to reconceptualize their future.

- Discover information. We allow participants to hear customers rage or talk to factory foremen on the floor. We encourage them to visit offices in other countries if the challenge is global. We also ask them to investigate and obtain published, legally and fairly obtained intelligence on the competition. Getting participants as close to the source of information as you can will increase the impact—impact that is needed for reconceptualization to take place.

Creating a parallel world of transformational learning.

- Do not hold Action Learning sessions on site. At least some of the time, removing participants from the world they know is important. Hold workshops in customers' offices, in other countries, in unusual learning contexts. People can absorb new information when they realize that this process is going to be different, and putting them on unfamiliar ground helps foster that realization.

- Balance work on a business project with non-task metaphorical experiences in order to unleash emotional energy. Give participants the chance to explore their feelings and attitudes through team-building exercises, outdoor adventures, break-through volunteer experiences, and discussions about individual behaviors. For many people, interpersonal growth is a prerequisite for reconceptualizing, and these non-business activities foster that growth. Action Learning can produce profound personal distress about one's values and life-distress that can be a catalyst to new leadership insights and behavior.

- Remove the usual restrictions. Team leaders, facilitators, coaches, and sponsors must communicate to participants that they are expected to transcend restrictive policies and parochial politics. For instance, many company cultures have unwritten rules about expressing opinions in areas outside of one's own function; or there may be negative consequences for anyone who challenges a CEO-mandated tactic or favorite consultant—including those who are delivering the Action Learning process. When all of these restrictions are removed, the barriers against revolutionary thinking are also taken away.

Constructively confronting people with their behaviors and beliefs.

- Provide strong feedback. Make sure feedback is a recurring part of any Action Learning program. That means feedback from coaches, the sponsor, and other participants. Team-on-team feedback is another possibility. Before someone reconceptualizes, she needs to be aware of her current viewpoint—an awareness that is often fostered by people's reactions to what she says and does in Action Learning sessions. At Ameritech, the lack of feedback in the culture was countered in the workshop design—participants were required to rate and evaluate each other. Feedback interventions should address the company's deficiencies.

- Challenge, confront, and contest. By feedback, we do not mean saying, "That's an interesting idea, though it seems a little hard to implement." Helping an individual deal with his behaviors and beliefs means saying, "I don't agree with your idea. I don't see how we could make your idea work even if we had unlimited time and money." We're not saying feedback has to be insulting. It should, however, be direct and revealing. Coaches can set the tone for this feedback and model it for participants.

- Focus on the "why." Force participants to explain why they refuse to entertain an innovative suggestion or why they continue to support archaic policies. In many workplaces, people are not challenged to explain their personal "whys." Here they do.

Building a theory of the case.

- Analyze the factors behind rethinking the business. Reconceptualization is not just a personal revelation; it requires data-gathering and analysis. Good coaches blend this analysis with leadership issues; they encourage participants to integrate their analysis with individual viewpoints on the business; they develop a point of view that can be articulated and defended to others.

- Raise the hard questions. Nothing develops a theory of the case faster than probing, pointed inquiries about why things are happening—especially if they are negative. Forcing participants to come to grips with why a cash-cow product is running dry or why people are leaving facilitates development of a theory.

Providing an environment in which a vision can emerge.

- Encourage visionary thinking. Coaches and facilitators push people to think like strategists rather than implementers. Given that they have been assigned a strategic project—one that makes them privy to information and thinking at the highest corporate level—they should respond to encouragement to think big and into the future.

- Suggest "what if" scenarios. Participants often become stuck in current realities; they offer reasons why something is unlikely or impossible (not enough money, time, etc.). Encourage speculation. Allow discussions to move out of the present into the hypothetical future. "What if we had unlimited resources, then. . . ."

8

Releasing Fresh Thinking and Independent Action

One of the imperatives of modern leadership is the ability to think and act independently based on the needs of the situation and the direction of the business. The bureaucratic leader who thinks and acts as she is told or as she expects the organization wants her to act is outdated. Unfortunately, if you dig below the surface of many companies, you will find outdated leaders (including those who are far too young to have developed such stodgy perspectives). Numerous forces conspire to keep the bureaucratic mindset in place and discourage independent and interdependent thinking and action.

Part of the problem is that managers are receiving mixed messages. Management communicates that they want their people to take risks, to be decisive, be innovative, forget tradition, and create a new tradition. At the same time, systems are in place in which the predominant leadership model promotes those who manage upward, avoid any serious mistakes, and keep their particular process running smoothly and predictably. As a rule, organizations abhor unpredictability.

These mixed messages confuse leaders. They may dip a toe in uncharted waters, but they are unwilling or unable to take the plunge. To help emerging leaders develop a passion for independent action and fresh thinking, organizations need to define both a leadership model and behaviors that will facilitate this action and thinking in their organizations and build an Action Learning program around them.

Discover and Define Your
Own Leadership Competencies

The model for leaders at General Electric is different from those at Johnson & Johnson. Although there are some similarities, the distinct culture of each organization shapes the requirement mix. Simply to borrow the leadership model of another organization and slap it on your own is impossible.

At General Electric, three key leadership competencies are speed, simplicity, and self-confidence. These are the qualities that will help each new generation of G.E. leaders move quickly and decisively, sort through complex technological and global issues, and make decisions without second-guessing themselves or worrying whether they have every last bit of information before they act. The model was defined by the CEO. At Johnson & Johnson, leadership competencies include managing paradox and complexity, independent partnering, focusing on the customer, competing, and innovating. This model was developed by a team of top-line managers and is used in all Action Learning programs. Merck places great emphasis on creating effective interpersonal relationships.

These models are the basis for an Action Learning process, and what it is designed to impart. As you can see, they are not skills that can be imposed on individuals through traditional lecture-and-manual training programs. They need to be developed within and emerge as part of an internalized learning process.

Notice that these leadership models flow from an organization's values. If successfully inculcated among leaders, these competencies help differentiate a company; they tell others what they can expect when dealing with Johnson & Johnson. For example, they also provide a way of building a distinct culture, of making sure that values and beliefs are communicated and instilled.

All this gives leaders a basis for action and independent thinking. They provide certainty and unanimity about what is important to a company. Whereas leaders may face ambiguous situations, there is no ambiguity about the values and behaviors sanctioned by the organization.

At G.E., for instance, very specific behaviors were encouraged in Action Learning programs, behaviors that emanated from the competencies of speed, simplicity, and confidence. Those behaviors were

- Have a passion for excellence and hate bureaucracy
- Have the self-confidence to involve everyone and behave in a boundaryless fashion
- Create a clear, simple, reality-based vision
- Have enormous energy and the ability to energize others
- Stretch, set aggressive goals, reward progress yet understand accountability and commitment
- See change as an opportunity and not a threat
- Have global brains and build diverse and global teams

At BellSouth, the model is different. The challenge that leaders face is to unite diverse parts of the organization (wireless and wire-live) into an integrated team working for the customer. The Action Learning process is focusing on adaptive leadership—that is, finding new ways to solve problems that involve and include people in the solution.

Making quick decisions and taking risks is much easier when there is no confusion about the behaviors, competencies, and values that the organization deems important. As you will see, Action Learning creates an environment in which learning about, challenging, and practicing these behaviors takes place.

Helping Leaders Discover How They Feel and What They Think

More than anything else, Action Learning offers people the opportunity to explore their feelings and beliefs. Part of an Action Learning workshop might involve a physical activity such as scaling a wall, racing cars, or visiting an AIDS clinic. This activity tells participants a great deal about how they feel about risk. Feedback from one's team forces individuals to confront why they are so reluctant to challenge a departmental norm to achieve an organizational goal.

Leaders cannot act decisively when they are not in touch with their feelings and beliefs. They lack the internal security necessary to state their opinion or make a decision that runs counter to conventional wisdom. Companies usually do not give people the chance to explore what they really feel. In fact, the "correct" pejorative is to label something too "touchy-feely" as the ultimate putdown. Companies do not often allow managers to investigate whether their personal beliefs are in accord with organizational values. Action Learning offers them that chance.

An Action Learning process starts by defining an issue for participants and asking them to take a position on it. It is not like a typical training scenario in which people are given the facts or a prevailing theory and then instructed on how they should use the information. Instead, they are introduced to a problem, opportunity, threat, or an issue sponsoring management feels is critical to address. At Ameritech, it was the immediate threat of deregulation. At Tektronix, it was redefining the core business. At NationsBank, it was the long-term concern about new ways to achieve growth, other than acquisition. At BellSouth, it was finding integrated customer solutions. Participants are forced to examine their role relative to this issue:

- What do they believe about the situation?

- Do they accept the premise that change is necessary to deal with the situation? If not, why not?

- What role have they had in perpetuating the current situation?

- How have they maintained the status quo in their managerial or leadership roles, and how has that helped create the current situation?

There is a certain "shock" value in confronting leaders with serious issues and their personal roles and beliefs relative to those issues. At Shell Oil, Action Learning groups were stunned to learn that, overall, their oil business was not returning the cost of capital. The news redefined their view of themselves and the historical position of a huge energy company. Grappling with that bit of information, which was not easily accepted, caused each participant to think long and hard about their assumptions about the business. Similarly, the Action Learning teams at the breakthrough leadership program at Ameritech for 120 change agents—held as new competitors were emerging and deregulation was being debated in Washington, D.C.— were at a loss to describe the telecommunications environment in five years. Most of the participants had not had much experience thinking about competition, the industry, and what the future would bring. Working for a company that had a lock on the market, they were not overly concerned about anything beyond pleasing the customer despite the cost, serving their bosses, and moving up the ladder. In the initial workshops, however, we confronted them with industry information and a learning process indicating that if they did not anticipate the future, the future was in jeopardy, because the competition certainly was doing so.

True bureaucrats can get by without having to take a strong personal position; they can simply fulfill the company position. Action Learning requires participants to take a position on important issues, and by doing so, begin to think for themselves about the business and the future.

When participants start receiving feedback, they are forced to examine their emotional and leadership armor for chinks. Feedback comes in many forms—they hear from other team members about their performance as leaders, they receive written evaluations, and they provide their own feedback through innovative devices. A group of Johnson & Johnson executives in Latin America have recently finished an Action Learning workshop in which they interviewed some of their key customers. Based on the data they received, they compiled a written analysis of themselves as leaders. They were told to be dispassionate, to analyze themselves as others might and write case studies of their leadership styles. They shared their reports with their Action Learning teams and acted as facilitators for a debate about themselves. What generally emerges from these sessions is illumination of blind spots. People discover their weaknesses as leaders, their Achilles heel as individuals, their prejudices and predispositions. A manager who thinks himself kind and tolerant discovers others view him as intolerant when his functional territory is invaded. Another executive who has always defined herself as a great motivator discovers that she sometimes comes off as pompous and patronizing.

Identifying these flaws and expanding one's self-awareness are more important than ever. Re-created leaders need to operate in an incredibly fast-paced, complex, and confusing world. People with large blind spots who are intolerant of learning about their impact on others find it difficult to function in a multicultural, ambiguous business world. They make mistakes because of these flaws, and their inability to adjust their behavior to the environment makes them indecisive and risk-averse. Re-created leaders are certainly not perfect. The Action Learning process, however, makes participants aware of their vulnerabilities and vigilant against the negative impact on others, while increasing their emotional intelligence and self-awareness.

The Opportunity to Act

For many people, Action Learning provides the first environment in which they feel free to act independently and decisively. We have found that just by giving participants a taste of this freedom they learn to relish it. Action Learning sets up situations in which participants are freed from the functional, creative, and political constraints of the workplace. They are encouraged to state their opinions, confront, provide honest feedback, and challenge themselves and others. They are also empowered. Participants recognize that they are not off on some academic exercise but that they have been given the power to influence the organization. This realization imbues the experience with meaning; it shows them what they can achieve when given this power and independence.

In 1996, Team Challenge at Citibank empowered three teams of potential leaders to make recommendations that could alter Citibank's business processes. The Action Learning format called for these teams to travel around the world, looking at the business as a strategic whole (rather than from their usual functional perspective), collecting information, and analyzing it. At the end, teams met with Citibank CEO John Reed and communicated their findings and recommendations. These were not typical presentations. The Action Learning process pushed participants to be direct and honest; this carried over into their presentations to Reed. They discussed and debated their findings; some engaged in what might be called "spirited disagreement" with the CEO. In early 1997, the teams were asked to repeat their presentations at Citibank's business directors' meeting.

When they were done, most of the participants had learned that nothing terrible happened when they stood up for their beliefs and fought for their recommendations. In fact, they felt like they had accomplished something important. The Team Challenge members had gone through an emotional and intellectually rigorous process and emerged with a much better sense of themselves and their business beliefs.

We have seen people emerge with this independence and confidence in every Action Learning program. Part of this comes from asking people to tackle issues they have never worked on before. At Johnson & Johnson, one Action Learning workshop had executives focus on change projects that advanced learning in their own companies. They were working way beyond their traditional functional boundaries, struggling with issues such as individual learning styles and barriers to learning within the Johnson & Johnson culture. The mere act of becoming more multidimensional in their thinking helped participants become different types of leaders.

At Shell Oil, teams were told to take on a project that would "grow revenues or cut costs." For the emerging leaders on these teams, this assignment seemed impossible. The time frame for the project was deemed too short and the expectations were considered too imprecise. Many felt they were already working on the most important priorities for the business. How could these possibly be redefined or rearranged? Most of the Shell leaders had never been given such a broad mandate; they were accustomed to assignments confined to their respective functions, developed after many interactions. Now they were thrown into a project where they needed to demonstrate multidimensional skills to succeed—and deliver immediate, measurable outcomes as well.

All this is not to say that every Action Learning team creates brilliant strategies in response to highly challenging assignments (though a number of them do). The experience of attacking an issue in a way they have never done before and finding new ideas and solutions is profound. Broadening their business view and achieving a difficult objective as a team gives participants the certainty that there is more than one way to run a business.

What Happens When You Throw These Action Learning Graduates Back into the System

Put another way, what happens when you return someone ready for action, eager to implement fresh ideas, and experienced with interacting with the CEO, back on a team with people who have not been to the mountaintop? Many times, good things happen. We have seen Action Learning graduates do a tremendous job disseminating a new leadership philosophy to direct reports and peers; we have seen their willingness to take risks and stand up for their beliefs greatly benefit teams, departments, and organizations; in the process, they have become permanent change agents.

Sometimes, however, there are tensions. It is important to be aware of some situations that develop, such as this example from a current client: Bill had been through Action Learning and it had encouraged his very positive qualities. He is a recognized leader in the company and is great at getting results and moving projects forward quickly—an entrepreneur—terrific at seizing on ideas and pushing them through the system, even if some people are rubbed the wrong way. But Bill is not perfect, and the Action Learning workshop did not change that fact. Like many entrepreneurs, he has a tendency to be dogmatic about his positions and usually prioritizes results over Johnson & Johnson values rather than seeking a balance between the two. In receiving 360-degree feedback in an Action Learning workshop, this blind spot was identified.

Jay (not his real name) joined Johnson & Johnson and reported to Bill in a key position. Jay is likable, process-oriented, team-friendly, politically correct, adaptable, and a good listener. After a short time, Bill decided to fire Jay. Jay had failed to launch new products, establish partnerships with medical institutions, or stand up for his beliefs. In Bill's view, he clearly demonstrated that he lacks original ideas, does not like challenging the system, and is too process-focused. When Bill brought up the topic of removing Jay, his boss and others in the company came down hard on him. "Can't he develop Jay? Is Bill so driven and focused on results that he cannot cut Jay a little slack? Is Jay's behavior a response to Bill's leadership?"

With the benefit of time and perspective, we can say that Bill was correct; he should have moved Jay on, at least transferring him. Jay was not going to change, no matter what anyone said or did. Bill's power to act was constrained by other people's fear of action. No doubt, sometimes Bill acted rashly and needed to be constrained. In this instance, however, he had wrestled with the issue and concluded that Jay was not helping the business. Unfortunately, the prevailing managerial mentality in even the most enlightened companies is to wait-and-see and conform to norms; fear of litigation adds to this tendency. Although organizations recognize in theory how important it is to have decisive, action-oriented leaders, bureaucratic constraints and legitimate legal concerns can inhibit them.

Here is another example of how Action Learning alumni create discomfort. Jack is a line manager who was transferred to human resources with the mandate to "shake it up" and make it more business-oriented. He had a reputation as someone who was highly proficient at meeting deadlines, coming up with productive ideas, and making processes more results-focused. Jack eschewed politics in favor of straight talk and a strong set of values. When Jack began to shake up HR, however, he offended people. At this organization (and at many others), HR can resist change in subtle and effective ways. HR can become concerned whether someone is being treated fairly or whether a sufficient number of people have been consulted before a decision is made. When Jack attempted to make HR more results-oriented, he violated the department's mini-culture and encountered a legion of consultants who were willing to help him overcome his inability to influence the HR functions effectively or to garner support. For instance, people were upset when he excluded some key executives from the decision-making chain in order to accelerate the process. Jack ended up firing them all and began to rebuild from the beginning.

The point of both these stories is not that companies should give people like Jack and Bill carte blanche to do what they please. Sometimes their propensity to act quickly and think later is detrimental. We include these stories here to illustrate the complexity of organizational change. Although Action Learning is a useful method to address leadership in business dilemmas, sometimes new ones can be created. It takes time for organizations to break with tradition or implement new leadership programs—and Action

Learning can cause new forms of resistance. Various employees, especially those who feel left out, can become nervous. Expect some clashes between Action Learning graduates who are energized by what is possible and empowered by the need to act and others who have not had the same experience and are confused by the new passion and sense of urgency in their leader.

Corporate cultures are shifting gradually so that change, speed, innovation, global thinking, and risk-taking are the norm. Action Learning can contribute to this shift but can also produce equally strong resistance. The more participants of Action Learning a given organization has, the less that resistance will be. That is the reason that companies such as Johnson & Johnson, Shell Oil, Ameritech, and others are utilizing the process at different levels of the organization; each layer of leadership subsequently influences another.

Providing an Environment Where Leaders Can Take Action

Not everyone is capable of becoming a decisive doer, of fighting against the tide. To paraphrase an old saying: If everyone were born to lead, who would follow? Every company must be aware that people's capacity for action varies greatly. Action Learning cannot transform a cautious bureaucrat into a risk-taking entrepreneur.

What Action Learning does is give people who have the potential to become change agents and leaders the opportunity to develop that potential. Companies today cannot benefit from a training program designed to reinforce prevailing attitudes—there will always be enough people willing to conform and maintain the status quo—but when a business strategy requires it, nurturing individuals' capacities to act and lead needs to be encouraged and developed. We have found that this is often a latent capacity, hidden from others until a temporary but demanding and encouraging environment in an Action Learning program brings it to the surface.

Not everyone who experiences Action Learning emerges as an independent-thinking risk-taker or potential CEO. When the compensation and promotion systems of companies still reward people who make the fewest mistakes, there is significant motivation to reduce risk rather than become active. Still, a significant percentage of people who experience Action Learning design are transformed emotionally, not simply intellectually. They are inspired by how much can be accomplished if they act from their heart, define a vision, and do what they believe, regardless of whether or not it is politically or culturally correct. Once they gain the satisfaction of speaking their minds and seeing their own ideas inspire others, they find it difficult to return to their formerly quiescent managerial mindsets. In a few cases, they must either change roles or leave the company. Often, a personal transformation is precipitated that carries over into other areas of life and career. This is the price of unlocking passion and commitment in potential leaders.

Actions and Learnings

Fresh thinkers and independent action-takers emerge when they are clear about the leadership model favored by their organizations and are encouraged to exhibit behaviors in line with those competencies. How do you set up an Action Learning scenario that achieves this goal? The following five-step process might help:

1. Given where your organization hopes to be in five years, identify the critical leadership skills and behaviors that will help it get there. There is a canon of leadership texts and gurus to assist in this task. In our experience, however, the best leadership models are developed internally by line executives who combine the elements of current success with the demands of the future.

2. Focus your model on two or three key leadership attributes by eliminating the ones your organization already has in abundance or the ones that seem of secondary importance.

3. Define a list of desired behaviors that flow from each attribute.

4. Identify a business project that requires leaders to exhibit those behaviors in order to complete the project successfully.

5. Design a learning process that allows people to experiment with, model, and receive feedback on those behaviors.

Once the project begins, coaches and sponsors focus on these behaviors. It takes a bit of time before people develop the confidence necessary to act in new ways. Typically, they have to think in new ways first.

The following questions will help provoke fresh thinking. You may use them directly with teams or individuals or indirectly.

- What obstacles stand in the way of achieving the goals of our business project?

- In a typical work situation in our company and culture, why is it difficult or impossible to remove those obstacles?

- What skills does it take to remove them?

- Do you have those skills; do you think you could develop them?

- What risks will you have to take to complete the project successfully; what will give you the confidence to take that risk?

- How would a traditional manager go about dealing with this project; how will you deal with it in the opposite way?

- What if you had no choice but to move the project forward immediately; what if the survival of the company—not to mention your job—depended on your coming up with a viable recommendation today and implementing it tomorrow? In this case, what would you recommend?

Giving Action Learning participants a chance to see the positive results of what they do during the process is especially important. Once they realize that good things happen when they think and act independently, they are likely to begin self-reinforcing. The following are some suggestions of what you might want to weave into the Action Learning program:

- Give participants an opportunity to present their recommendations to a top executive; let them experience the excitement and career risks of making a bold, innovative proposal. They must prepare for the presentation by analyzing their target, determining the political positions involved, and selecting the compelling arguments.

- Make sure there is a follow-up process in place, that recommendations are acted upon by management within a reasonable time frame, and that participants hear the results.

- If recommendations are approved, give the members who made the recommendations a chance to help implement them or make a clear hand-off to another team or individual who will carry the recommendations forward.

- Even if recommendations are not approved, provide participants with feedback about both why they were not accepted and the positive things that came out of their work. Coaches and sponsors should encourage people to continue those positive behaviors.

- Identify people who exhibit innovative leadership and independent action-taking, and reward them.

9

For Companies to Learn to Change, People Must Learn to Change

I n many of the case histories and examples cited throughout this book, the need for change has been an underlying theme. It is not as though this need for change is new; even the old sweat shop bosses probably instituted new processes and policies that required adjustments. Today, however, the pace of change has escalated, requiring people to make huge shifts in behavior. Management does not just want its people to evolve over time; they want and need them to change *now*. They are especially concerned about emerging leaders' attitudes and behaviors related to change. If a company's leaders are not change agents and champions of new cultural imperatives, how can the company expect the rank and file to make major shifts in the way they work? It all boils down to this:

The ability of organizations to change has become inextricably linked to the ability of individual employees to change.

Over the years, Action Learning has helped many companies communicate and capitalize on this linkage. In the real world, months or even years might pass before individuals understand and embrace an organization's change initiative. In the temporary system of Action Learning, these changes occur in a matter of weeks. The intensity of the process, the team framework, the coaching, the high-stakes presentations to the company's leaders—all combine to make rapid individual and strategic transformations possible.

Getting People to Change Is a Lot Harder Than It Looks

People do not resist change in the way commonly assumed. So much has been written about change management, change agents, paradigm shifts, and new competition that most managers recognize that change is necessary. If you go into an organization, you will find people readily agreeing that they need to shift from a pyramid to a flat organizational structure, from an individual focus to teams, from one market to the next. When it comes to accepting intellectually the need for external change, resistance is usually minimal. When the changes are internal, however, problems arise.

A large benefits consulting firm is going through an Action Learning process as of this writing, attempting to use the process to define and ultimately change their culture. During the initial workshop, participants talked excitedly about how they needed to create a new policy here and adopt a new set of values there. They discussed everything they wanted to change—except themselves. This is how resistance occurs.

Resistance also occurs when change "demands" things of people. Most managers feel overwhelmed dealing with the ever-escalating requirements of their jobs. When they are asked to spend time learning a new skill, adapting to a new procedure, or spending countless hours developing others, they resist, perhaps covertly. To them, change is a time-consuming pain they would rather not endure.

Sometimes, too, people do not see the linkage between internal and external changes. They do not recognize that for the organization to become more global, individuals will need to abandon their local mindsets and make difficult decisions that only make sense on a worldwide basis, or that involve tradeoffs that might inhibit local growth.

There are also, of course, those who rationalize why they do not or will not change. Perhaps the most common rationalization is to indict one's boss or the company's leadership: "If only management would . . ., then I would." Rather than confront and overcome their own fears of changing the status quo, they deny they are afraid by blaming someone else.

Books have been written about the complexity of managing change, and we are not going to get bogged down in a discussion of why this is the case. What is important to understand, however, is that helping people to change is complex, difficult, and sometimes impossible. As we shall see, Action Learning can move people along the path. As the next section suggests, many change management programs do not.

There Is Nothing Rational About It

Some companies seem routinely to post sign-up sheets for the latest change initiative. They believe that if people understand what the change is all about and then make a commitment, behaviors will follow. That works with some issues, but most behavior is not a rational or linear process.

Judging from most change management workshops, however, one would think behavioral change was a logical, linear process. Some experts cite case histories about how other organizations have changed; they present compelling reasons why a given organization has to be transformed; they provide step-by-step instructions on "what you can do to make change happen." In some cases, "change models" are provided, as though organizations and people adhere to predetermined models.

If change did not have messy emotional and psychological components, change management texts and workshops would be very effective. Think about how difficult it is to stop smoking, lose weight, adopt a regular exercise program, or make any sort of significant personal change. It is difficult because there are many complex, sometimes unconscious, issues involved. The same is true within organizations. People need to debate the issues; they have to work through their feelings; they need to make commitments and practice new behaviors; they require verbal reinforcement; they need new knowledge and skills to make change happen; they must bring covert and unconscious cultural issues to the surface; they must experience an epiphany of sorts to see how their own personal change can drive strategic organizational change; they must develop a theory of the case as to why and how change happens. Action Learning facilitates these reactions and revelations.

Working Through the Bad News

Many Action Learning programs begin with an attention grabber. Participants gather in a workshop and are initially surprised at what they see and hear. Through the words of the company's leaders, via interviews with key industry people, and thorough a variety of other mediums, participants face harsh realities. Many times, these realities come in the form of bad news.

At Shell, Action Learning was a forum to alert managers that the company must improve and could obtain a better return through passbook savings. At Ameritech, an Action Learning process communicated that deregulation meant the end of a comfortable era and the beginning of an uncertain future. Action Learning sets up an environment ideal for delivering bad news and helping people work through it. At both Shell and Ameritech, early team meetings allowed participants to share their feelings about the changes their companies were confronting. Some people were very angry—they expressed their resentment that things had to change and looked for someone to blame, even the consultants, who "had it wrong." Others expressed their fears: of a deregulated future, a new culture, losing their jobs, being forced to fire people, being able to adjust to new leadership requirements; of the uncertain future. In a sense, participants were working through a grieving process, moving through the stages of shock, denial, anger, bargaining, and acceptance.

The ability to vent personal feelings within a structured, team setting is one reason people come to accept changes occurring within their organizations. Equally important, however, is the ability to do something about those changes. Action Learning is more than group therapy or a chance to vent frustrations. It allows participants to do something about their uncomfortable new circumstances. More specifically, it empowers and requires them to do something about it. Change is tough to handle when it is imposed and causes people to feel powerless. It is much easier to handle when you can exert an influence over what happens in a changing organization.

Action Learning always revolves around real work projects. It mandates that participants present project recommendations to top management and/or business group heads, and the process requires that these recommendations are taken seriously and enacted if management finds them to be solid.

Another Action Learning ingredient is helping participants to construct their own theory of the case. How does change happen? Why does it happen? When people develop their own perspective on change in their companies, it no longer seems like something bad and unmanageable. In a typical Action Learning workshop, participants learn about change in other settings and companies, they hear about different change management ideas, and they get the chance to test new behaviors and strategies related to the projects they are working on. From all this, they formulate their own ideas about change. Developing a theory of the case is especially important for a company's emerging leaders. They will lead change initiatives in the future, and they'll be much better equipped to do so if they have constructed their own theory of how to make it happen. In the process of re-creation, leaders begin to look at the world differently. They stop taking traditional explanations as gospel and begin developing their own ideas about the way things work. This is especially true when it comes to change.

One of the Biggest Change Initiatives in Corporate History, Part I

The Action Learning program at General Electric took many forms. The one we describe here was an early version of Action Learning and lacks some of the tools and elements of the later forms. Still, it is a great illustration of how Action Learning helps a company and its employees deal with the problems that accompany change.

By 1987, CEO Jack Welch had downsized G.E.'s workforce from 425,000 to 270,000 employees. He had eliminated layers of bureaucracy and levels of management. He had also launched his strategy of being number one or two in each of G.E.'s thirteen business areas or "fixing, selling, or closing" any business that came up short. These structural and strategic goals had largely been achieved by 1987. The culture, however, still was mired in the past. Welch's plan was to create a boundaryless organization characterized by values such as speed, simplicity, and self-confidence. Openness and communication would be hallmarks of this new culture and bureaucracy would be the enemy. Ultimately, employees would become more productive because of the opportunities presented by this type of environment.

Unfortunately, many G.E. employees responded to the downsizing, restructuring, and other major changes with fear and distrust. They worried that another downsizing might be in the offing; they were exhausted rather than excited by the changes taking place around them; they were less honest and open in their communications than ever before.

In the following months, G.E.'s Crotonville staff and outside consultants met to discuss how to energize and excite 270,000 employees about the new work paradigm. By spring of 1988, they had settled on what came to called "Work Outs" designed to take out unnecessary work from the system. Because of the downsizing and other changes, people were upset and frustrated by the overwhelming amount of work to be done. The idea was that if unnecessary work could be eliminated, people would have the time and inclination to participate and become part of the new policies, procedures, and strategies. Work Outs, however, had a more subtle but no less important purpose: to give people a sense of the changed organization's possibilities. Once employees saw for themselves the benefits of open communication, a boundaryless structure, and increased participation, they would change their behaviors and help change the organization.

Work Outs were "town meetings" of between 40 and 120 people. These meetings were actually two-and-a-half-day workshops that started with a session with business heads. They briefed the groups on their purpose—to come up with a recommendation to eliminate unnecessary reports, approvals, meetings, measurements, policies, and procedures. As in all Action Learning programs, participants were given the chance to have a major impact on the business. The ground rules were laid out from the start: Business heads would take every recommendation seriously and either say "yes" immediately, reject it, or agree to study it further and give participants a date for a decision. Furthermore, with every accepted recommendation, a timetable for implementation would be laid out.

From the very beginning, participants realized they were not engaged in an academic exercise. For many of them, this was an unprecedented chance to participate in decision making that had a major impact on the company.

As important as it was to eliminate unnecessary work, it was equally important that participants adapt and learn to function in the new business environment. The Work Out sessions encouraged this adaptation and learning in a number of ways. First, each group consisted of a multilevel, multifunction, multilocation mix of employees. It mirrored the boundaryless organization Welch wanted to create. For the first time, titles and functional responsibilities meant nothing. Suddenly, people explored the possibilities of a new way of working and found that it was energizing.

At the beginning of the Work Out sessions, people were split into teams of between seven and nine people and outside consultants served as coaches and facilitators, helping participants learn team-building and idea-generating skills. Then they began meeting and working on recommendations. At the end of Work Outs, teams presented their recommendations to the business heads.

One of the Biggest Change Initiatives in Corporate History, Part II

As you can imagine, Work Outs did not help 200,000-plus people change their attitudes and behaviors overnight. Still, given the number of people involved, it happened pretty damn fast. Part of the reason it happened fast was that the Action Learning process can easily be shaped to meet an organization's evolving requirements. In G.E.'s case, the next step in the evolution was to focus the process on the "low-hanging fruit." People needed to understand that the new culture, strategy, and structure of G.E. was not just about reducing the amount of unnecessary work; it meant a new way of dealing with business problems and opportunities.

For example, G.E. Power Systems had just lost a bid to a competitor on the sale and installation of power generating equipment. A group of G.E. engineers got together and decided to hold a Work Out session over a weekend, inviting people at all levels and from all functions to participate. The goal was to see whether they could find ways to reduce their costs in order to make more competitive bids on this type of equipment. The session was held, a number of ideas were presented and implemented, and shortly thereafter G.E. won a major project. Word spread quickly throughout G.E., and people became excited about the possibilities of the new paradigm. Other, similar Work Out sessions demonstrated that G.E. really was empowering its people to make major decisions.

Action Learning then moved to another stage. One of Welch's concerns was that the company was overly dependent on outside consultants to orchestrate the Work Out sessions. His goal was to make a transition from external consultants to internal change agents. In other words, he wanted G.E.'s leadership to assume responsibility for championing change.

With this goal in mind, G.E. launched its Change Acceleration Process (CAP). Unlike the Work Outs, CAP focused on "intact" teams—teams that existed within G.E. and were working on specific change issues. Some were grappling with growth strategies; others were attempting to increase diversity in the workforce. CAP gave them the opportunity to address these issues in a different way. It set up an Action Learning environment in which new ideas and behaviors related to the targeted issues could be explored and tested.

Through three formal workshops and informal meetings following the workshops, teams were introduced to the G.E. Model for Change. This three-part model consisted of the following (each part was taught at a workshop):

- Initiating change (leading, creating a shared need, and shaping a vision)

- Leveraging change (mobilizing commitment)

- Making it last (committing to the action plan, monitoring progress, and using systems/structures to institutionalize change)

The idea was that participants would learn the model and then have a chance to apply it to their particular change issues. The learning was focused on the workshops, the action focused on the meetings between workshops.

Though Action Learning remains an ongoing process at G.E. (with many other wrinkles, some of which have been discussed in previous chapters), the organization has undergone a massive transformation that has helped it maintain and widen its lead in most markets. Certainly the success of this process is reflected in G.E.'s glowing balance sheet, but it is also reflected in a unique measurement system Welch created. It consists of a simple chart. A number of traits are listed—traits that G.E. wants to see more of and less of in its people. Here is that chart:

More of:

- Initiating

- Seeking results

- Making proposals

- Solving problems

- Asking and listening

- Looking everywhere for answers

- Being empowered by what they influence

- Making it happen for themselves

Less of:

- Responding

- Seeking permission

- Making recommendations

- Complaining about problems

- Telling

- Looking upward for answers and solutions

- Being limited to what they control

- Letting it happen to them

Actions and Learnings

Can Action Learning help your organization deal with its particular change obstacle or issue? One way to start answering that question is by figuring out what has gone wrong in the past. Look at the following list and see whether you recognize any of the following:

The Five Errors Committed by Change-Devoted Companies

1. Focusing on external strategies to facilitate change and ignoring internal ones.

2. Assuming people are change-resistant when they are actually overwhelmed by their jobs and fear the additional demands on their time that a change initiative requires.

3. Failing to make the connection between individual and organizational change.

4. Managing change as a rational, linear process.

5. Not giving people the opportunity to confront and conquer the emotional and psychological issues raised by change.

Another way to evaluate your approach to change is by asking the following questions. As you can see, they help you think about whether you have applied the principles of Action Learning to your change efforts:

- Have you given your people the opportunity to debate, talk about their fears, and express their resentment related to the changes the company is going through?

- Do your people feel empowered or powerless when it comes to organizational change?

- Have your managers—especially the company's future leaders—developed their own sense of what makes change happen?

- Do people offer excuses about why they cannot make mandated changes; do they blame the company or their bosses for their inability to change?

- Has the organization given people a chance to try out new behaviors and approaches; are people given opportunities to go about projects in a different way in a supportive environment?

Let us assume for the moment that you want to use Action Learning to help your organization deal with a critical change issue. Before moving forward, see if all the necessary checklist items are in place:

The Change Checklist for Action Learning

1. Identify the major change the organization needs to make (the new strategic direction the business should take).

2. Identify the individual behaviors and attitudes that will help the organization make this change (or move in the desired strategic direction).

3. Find projects that will link individual behaviors/attitudes with organizational change (and that can be used within an Action Learning program).

4. Select participants who are considered crucial to the company's change initiative and who may have an impact on leading the company in a new direction.

5. Choose an Action Learning sponsor who feels strongly about the change initiative and will support it from start to finish.

10

Fusing Technology and the Business

In the last year or two, we have worked with an increasing number of organizations directing Action Learning efforts at technology-related issues. At first, the process might not seem to fit the purpose. Why would a company need Action Learning to figure out whether it should make an investment in a new computer system? Would the engineers and MIS specialists not be in a better position to assess technological needs then multifunction Action Learning teams? The answer to these questions begins with a simple statement of fact:

Organizations are having enormous difficulty getting technology leaders to integrate the business issues and business leaders to integrate the technology issues.

CEOs and other top executives are frustrated by the inability of these two groups to think holistically. They are stymied by technocrats who devise cutting-edge systems that ignore the imperative of better business results. They are frustrated by managers who are unable or unwilling to assess technological trends and realities and how they dovetail with business strategies.

On top of the technophobia and technocratitis that plague many companies, there is a dearth of problem-solving, opportunity-seizing ideas—ideas that are an innovative blend of high-tech smarts and low-tech business acumen. It is difficult to get organizational leaders strategizing with both in mind. Even more difficult is sitting business and technology people down at the same table and having them talk the same language.

Action Learning offers an environment and the tools to overcome these difficulties. Now we look at how different organizations use them.

A Wide Range of Applications

Let us start off with a few brief descriptions of the technology issues companies have addressed with their Action Learning programs:

- *Johnson & Johnson* looked at how information technology is changing their selling proposition; how it influences methods of selling to both health care professionals and consumers.

- *Shell Oil* is focusing on how their information architecture might help them run the company in a far more decentralized fashion.

- *Ameritech* is concentrating on how they are going to give others access to their central network (as a result of deregulation) and which core technologies they need to keep.

- *NationsBank* is looking at how technology will change the basic relationship between bank and customer.

In these and other cases, the impulse to use Action Learning often comes from a need to get people thinking in new directions. These companies are also caught in past technology investments. They have invested huge amounts of money in mainframes and software that often were designed for highly centralized structures.

As they make the transition to decentralized structures, teams, and distributed work, some systems and architecture are no longer appropriate. Besides these internal issues, they are facing external challenges from new technologies that confer competitive product and service advantage and customer demands for certain processes and systems. How do they help the company make the transition to new technologies? How do they help their people close the technology gap between what they have and what they will need in the near future?

These questions demand a quantum leap both in thinking and in workplace behaviors. A few brainstorming sessions are not going to make that leap possible. At even its most basic level, Action Learning fosters a reassessment of assumptions. Just by putting technology and business strategists on the same team and letting them benchmark companies that have made a successful transition from old to new technologies, fresh perspectives are developed.

At Citibank, a recent Action Learning strategic mandate was to investigate how the bank could capitalize on the Internet. CEO John Reed and other top managers were acutely aware that other companies—especially companies outside the traditional banking arena—were eventually going to provide fierce competition through their Internet-delivered financial services. What could Citibank do about it?

The Team Challenge group knew a great deal about banking but precious little about Internet technologies. Their project revolved around how Citibank might profitably use the Internet. In addition, they were instructed *not* to look for solutions inside of the bank but outside of it; there were told to spend 70 percent of their time investigating what others were doing to capitalize on the Internet. As in all Action Learning programs, the team would make recommendations to top management about how to proceed.

They went out into the world of cyberspace and nonbanking companies and began examining a number of issues. In their meetings, they debated questions such as

- Who is really making money off the Internet?

- Is it possible that the Internet is much ado about nothing; that it is something we can dismiss?

- Who might be our next competitor outside of banking that capitalizes on the Internet?

- As bankers, what technologies should we be investing in now to take advantage of the Internet in the future?

- What companies have developed (or are developing) the technological tools that make transactions easy, accessible, fast, and cost-effective for Internet users?

Team members visited Silicon Valley companies and came back energized and brimming with thought-provoking concepts. Banking traditionalists have been lobbing terms like *servers* and *browsers* as if they were grenades; have produced an explosive debate within the organization that is being felt at all levels. Citibank is still working through many issues, but minds have been changed and new ideas are being explored. In many Action Learning programs, that is a paramount goal of the process. It also forces people to take a position on the issue. Remaining on the sidelines when something is unfamiliar or threatening is all too easy. The recommendations spawned by Action Learning force people to choose sides.

Action Learning programs are also a great way to surmount resistance or indifference to new technological applications. G.E. had been doing a great deal of R&D work for the Air Force in the area of artificial intelligence. One project involved using artificial intelligence to develop models that would help pilots make quick decisions. These models facilitated quick access to a great deal of data and decisions based on that data.

One of the people who had worked closely on developing this model thought the technology would transfer nicely to G.E. Capital. It would be useful for phone service representatives attempting to make decisions related to loans. But because the two areas were so different—loans and defense work were like proverbial apples and oranges—no one took this advocate's suggestion very seriously. Still, when a sponsor was found at G.E. Capital for an Action Learning program built around this issue (a sponsor that was found only after much searching), it offered the opportunity to try the project on an experimental basis. This experiment eventually blossomed into a database management tool that is essential for how G.E. qualifies loans and deals with many other customer service issues.

Reshaping Technology Dialogues, Attitudes, and Visions

Within the crucible of Action Learning, organizations have the opportunity to address a wide variety of technology-related issues. The intensity of the process, the pressure of making recommendations to top management, the high-impact projects, the diversity of the teams and the 360-degree feedback all catalyze a rethinking of long-held beliefs about technology. Prejudices, misconceptions, and fears are uncovered and worked through as part of the process, allowing companies to move toward a true integration of technology and business strategy.

Let us look at six common issues organizations address and the attitudes they reshape:

1. *Moving beyond automation and process redesign.* Within every organization, a significant percentage of managers view technology purely as automation, as "machines" that can save time and money. There is little vision to their perspective. They are not asking questions such as, "How will technology transform work and transform our future?" Action Learning can drive people toward these questions. Projects can put them in direct contact with companies where employees have unprecedented access to information, power, and choice

because of technology. They can articulate their fears about how this techno-future might change their jobs and their companies. Whatever the business mandate of their particular Action Learning program might be, it helps participants make the shift from technology as automation to technology as transformation.

2. *Turning on older managers to a high-tech world.* There is an invisible divide between a younger generation that was raised with computers and an older generation that grew up in a low-tech environment. For younger executives, computers represent more than something that they have to learn to use; they are comfortable with and adapt more easily to technology-driven changes. Action Learning helps older executives surface their phobias and provides a forum for younger and older executives to work together on technology-related issues. It also compresses the time required to feel comfortable with technology; the intensity and pressure of the workshops and team sessions accelerate high-tech socialization.

3. *Seeing the bigger picture.* Technology discussions often turn into cost-benefit analysis: If we invest x dollars in technology, we will get y benefits from it. That in turn translates to discussions about whether the company should purchase System A or B; whether they should pursue R&D or purchase a new technology to develop a higher quality product and reduce manufacturing costs. The problem with this cost-benefit mentality is that it limits options. It prevents people from exploring technological trends. It avoids projections of what might happen if a new technology catches on or how it might change customer requirements. Action Learning is a forum for big-picture thinking. It challenges participants to look beyond the quotidian cost-benefit analysis and explore new ideas and trends.

4. *Recognizing the new leadership possibilities.* One of the most fascinating aspects of Action Learning workshops is how partici-

pants come to see that a new style of leadership is not only possible but desirable. This often happens as people gather evidence of how technology diffuses power, connects diverse people, and moves information at shocking speeds. In this "distributed" environment, information moves away from the center toward the periphery. Customers and employees have far more knowledge than in the past. Within the learning environments of teams, managers see that their old command-and-control style is ill-suited to the new workplace that technology is creating.

5. *Dealing with hard cases.* In every company, we have experienced a minority of dyed-in-the-wool technophobes and technocrats. We have seen sales and marketing people who firmly believe that the technological revolution is irrelevant to their jobs; they only grudgingly consider how emerging processes and systems affect customer relationships. There are engineering and manufacturing leaders who are still caught up in system specs and do not leave their silos. We worked with one leader who was a brilliant engineer in the aircraft engine division of a major corporation. He had spent his working life thinking about things like turbine blades, and when the information systems division of his company developed a new way of delivering data to customers, he viewed it as an inconvenience (it required him to make process changes that he viewed as cumbersome and unnecessary). This engineer set up roadblock after roadblock to stop this new data delivery method from being implemented. When this engineer went through an Action Learning program, however, he was forced to confront his myopia. Others on his team pointed it out to him. He had to go out into the field and interview actual customers; the ability of the team to complete its mission successfully depended on his seeing the connection between technology and customers. Gradually, albeit grudgingly, the engineer's perspective shifted.

6. *Making what is overwhelming manageable.* Action Learning gives people the time, space, and setting to reflect on technology's impact. On a day-to-day work level, most people do not have time for this reflection. Overwhelmed by the demands of their jobs, they reflexively blame technology for all sorts of things: "The new system makes me do twice the amount of work to achieve the same end"; "The investment we're making in researching that new technology is going to cost us our bonuses." Technology is a convenient scapegoat for all the problems and stresses in the modern workplace. Action Learning puts technology in perspective. It lets people work on a project with teams that include pro-technology people. It encourages them to gather data from outside the company so they see different ways that technology influences how people do their jobs and how companies make money. Best of all, people can reflect on their discussions with team members, the feedback they have received from coaches, and how their biases about technology affect their work.

Actions and Learnings

Is your organization encountering the types of problems discussed in this chapter? To answer that question, ask yourself the following:

1. How often do your key business strategists, line executives, and technical people regularly meet to strategize about the future?

2. When they meet, do they talk the same language; do people respect each other's viewpoints, or do they merely present their own ideas without really listening?

3. Is there a technology generation gap in your company between younger and older employees?

4. When you have attended meetings to discuss issues such as Internet sites and new manufacturing technologies, does the dis-

cussion revolve around cost/benefit analysis or is it more far-reaching (do people share best practices from other companies, for instance)?

5. Do you consider your company's technology strategy a slave to a major investment it made in systems or processes years ago?

6. Do employees blame new systems for various problems they or the company are experiencing?

7. Are there technology-related opportunities that competitors are taking advantage of and your company is not (or is taking advantage of them too late)?

8. Is technology changing your workplace—the way power and information is distributed—and if so, does the leadership style of management reflect the changes?

Thinking about and discussing these questions will give you a good sense of whether Action Learning might be helpful in addressing the technology/business nexus that confounds many organizations. The next step is to take the following step-by-step approach to launch an Action Learning project in this area:

1. *Locate a sponsor.* Determine who in your organization recognizes the need to connect business strategy with technological vision. Make sure this prospective sponsor not only understands the issues involved but has the clout within the company to mandate that engineers and general business people work on teams together. (We have found that clout is key here, in that there is often resistance to mixing these two "opposing" groups.)

2. *Analyze which issues are of paramount concern.* Sometimes the issues are major and obvious. Ameritech, for instance, recognized that it had to shift its network executive's perspective on its core technologies because of deregulation. At other times, the issues are amorphous—a company fears that technology is reshaping its culture but no one is managing all the changes that

are occurring. Begin a dialogue with the sponsor about what key concerns he or she has.

3. *Focus Action Learning projects on a specific topic.* Given the general issue identified in the previous step, analyze what project best serves that issue. Is there a division that is particularly vulnerable to technological trends and are the people in that division technocrats or technophobes? Might Action Learning teams come up with new structures and procedures for a particular business unit that better fits a distributed workforce? Should teams focus on a particularly controversial new technology that is sure to engender heated debate and discussion; should their mission be to recommend whether or not the organization adopts this technology?

4. *Select participants based on the projects chosen.* The best Action Learning teams mix unlikely specialists—a sales executive and a systems engineer, for instance. Look for people who are highly proficient in their areas but do not see the big picture. It is also useful to evaluate who in the company will play a critical role in making future technology decisions. It may be that an organization wants to use Action Learning to determine who should be making those decisions. Action Learning can reveal a great deal about an individual's capacity for dealing with thorny problems in this area.

5. *Determine the tools and techniques that will work best given technology/business goals established.* If you want to shake participants up about their technological biases, an emphasis on 360-degree feedback might be warranted. If you feel your people need to develop a broader vision of what is possible, visits to standard-setting high-tech companies might be in order. In the technology arena especially, there are some brilliant outside speakers whom you might want to bring in to plant some seeds.

11

Removing the Barriers Between Customer and Company

Action Learning programs at General Electric, Johnson & Johnson, Citibank, Ameritech, NationsBank, and other companies all have had a customer focus. These companies have recognized that the customer-related issues they face cannot simply be addressed by marketing and sales specialists on an ad hoc basis. They have hired consultants to study their customer problems and present them with options, few of which were implemented. They have started to understand that their problems (not to mention their opportunities) go deeper than surface difficulties with customer service or distribution channels.

Time and again, we have found that organizational behaviors and attitudes filter the customer voice; or they distort that voice; or they respond to it through functional biases; or they hear only what they want to hear, locked into past customer service practices.

Action Learning helps reduce the misconceptions, re-creating leaders who are able to shift their thinking and strategies. It does so in many ways, but perhaps the most significant is the intense interaction between Action Learning participants and customers. Without that direct contact, people outside of marketing and sales rarely talk to customers or fully grasp the rapidly shifting issues and concerns that they have. Perhaps some managers grasp these issues intellectually, but they do not recognize the profoundly different concerns customers have now versus only a few years ago.

The extensive customer interviewing that is part of Action Learning opens many participants' eyes, some of whom have never visited customers at their locations. The insights and information participants bring back to Action Learning teams are used to challenge assumptions. People are forced to confront long-held beliefs that "customers care only about price" and "speed is the only important element of service."

From our experience leading customer-focused Action Learning workshops we have identified nine key themes—recurring themes that will give you a sense of what emerging leaders need to learn in order to enjoy productive and profitable relationships with their customers.

Nine Ways to Build Better Customer Relationships

Why do customers remain dissatisfied despite a company's best efforts to please those customers? Why are organizations hearing one thing from their sales force and another thing entirely from their customers? Why do customers feel as though a company does not understand them even though the company has spent untold amounts of money on market research to help them understand?

There are no easy answers to these questions. That is why some companies are baffled and confused by their own customers. "What do they want, anyway?" is sometimes heard in meeting rooms during the day and in bars afterward.

The good news is that deeper understanding and relations with customers can be fostered, but only if leadership recognizes emerging realities that sometimes are subtle and sometimes are hard to accept. These realities are our themes, so let us examine each of them:

- *A new type of customer with new requirements and resources.* Within internally focused corporate bureaucracies, the customer is an abstract concept—especially for staff groups. Many managers are removed from the "white-hot breath of the customer" and therefore are not aware of how different the customer of the past is from the customer of the present. In health care, HMOs have supplanted doctors and hospitals. In technology, the end-user is constantly shifting. In manufacturing, a handful of suppliers are replacing hundreds of suppliers as they form tight circles of reduced inventory and strong partnerships. On top of all this, Internet, Intranet, and Extranet are not only providing purchasing alternatives for customers, they are making more customer information available more quickly to more people—eliminating or redefining traditional distribution channels. Your new customers may be 15,000 miles away, but they have a world of information at their fingertips. Action Learning helps participants define who the company's customers are and who future customers will be, and it helps them discard expectations that are not relevant.

- *A customer cannot be managed.* Despite much that has been written about relationship selling, many senior executives believe that customers can be attracted and kept because of distinctive product features; that pricing strategies, brand loyalty programs, and other tactics alone can be used to satisfy customers. More so now than ever before, the real things that keep customers happy are dependability, truthfulness, integrity, corporate reputation, and mutual empathy. Building customer relationships is much more difficult than building distinctive products. In many Action Learning workshops, we have found that many executives view relationship selling as a sales technique. The shift we help them make is to view it as an organizational value to be honored. Both organizations and cultures hold collective views of "the customer." Once this view is challenged, participants begin respecting the customer in new ways and become more effective at establishing productive customer relationships and not as con-cerned about "controlling" customers. It may seem sim-ple but the route to getting there is challenging and requires learning about and seeing the customer differently.

- *Customers have goals too.* When participants start talk-ing about customers during Action Learning programs, they invariably refer to the importance of a "customer strategy that meets our company's goals." The cus-tomer's goals are minimized. To establish a meaningful partnership with customers, companies must define what customers are trying to achieve, who they are, and what drives them in that direction.

- *Challenge the business proposition.* We sell tires, we make mainframes, we are auditors. Organizations are some-times slow to redefine who they are in relationship to what customers really need. You make computers, but your customer really wants network solutions. It may be that your service, such as auditing, has become a commodity or that someone does it faster, better, or cheaper or that customers want it in a different form. Challenging the business proposition keeps companies in touch with customer needs, and it is something that is not done frequently enough. A company's core com-petence is achieved around its central business proposi-tion—who we are and how we add value.

- *Customers do not always know what they want.* An important misconception we have identified is that leaders listen and respond to customer needs. Re-created leaders not only listen and respond, they interpret and develop a theory of what customers will need. One of the skills we encourage Action Learning participants to develop is the ability to "read between the lines" and translate the values of a customer to a new product or service. Products such as cellular phones, VCRs, and disposable contact lenses were not developed in response to well-defined customer requirements. Instead, astute organizations interpreted the signals (vague as they sometimes might be), factored in customer values, and came up with products that were there before customers articulated that they needed them. Anticipation of a new market is more profitable than merely serving the current one, because the real profit advantage usually goes to those who arrive first.

- *Customer intimacy incentives.* Leaders provide incentives to salespeople to sell more and to keep sales costs down. This is the way it has always been, but it is no longer such a wise policy in a changing business environment. At Ameritech, CEO Dick Notebaert was incredulous when he heard the following story. A customer complained that when he asked a service rep who was installing a phone in his bedroom to install another phone in the kitchen, the service rep refused; he explained that the customer had to make another service request, and he would return tomorrow to install the second phone. The CEO wondered what kind of stupid bureaucratic rule resulted in this type of simple service mistake. In fact, the rule was designed to control costs; yet Ameritech was losing money, was virtually "giving away" service as service representatives spent countless hours honoring these types of requests. Centralized cost decisions like this one are not wrong, but they need to be balanced with long-term customer relationship concerns. Re-created leaders must find ways to strike that balance so that relationship-destroying situations like the one described above are not commonplace.

- *Distrust of customers.* Some leaders may not like to admit it, but there is sometimes a cynical sense that today customers are "out to get everything they can," which is brought about by escalating demands of customer-supplier partnerships. This leads to companies believing that the only way they can earn customer loyalty is through price, frequent user programs, and additional services. Although there is some truth in that belief, it also produces a distance from and wariness of the customer. Executives making decisions about customer programs may not directly experience customers often; they lack the visceral feel for what moves the customer. Sales teams may have that feel, but they have largely been disempowered in favor of cost efficiencies. New organizational leaders find a way to factor that visceral sense of the customer into their decision making and restore a more trusting relationship with customers.

- *Disempowered customer service representatives.* Many customer service representatives labor under adverse conditions. They often suffer poor morale, high turnover, and can be generally discouraged by their jobs. They have not been given the proper training, information, or policies to facilitate productive customer interactions, and yet they must bear the heat of customer dissatisfaction. In fact, management's adherence to the

80/20 rule (20 percent of the company's customers are responsible for 80 percent of the business) has sent the message that a minority of customers should receive first-class service whereas the majority is not worth that effort. The service value chain depends on customer service employees recognizing that the company's service philosophy is not often this black and white. Leaders still need to put policies and programs in place that motivate people to want to serve the majority of customers better and empower them to do so. This is a never-ending challenge in business today.

- *The Internet eliminates the middlemen.* The Internet economy that is currently evolving will produce an immediate link between buyer and seller, ending traditional roles of distribution, pricing, aggregate marketing, and so on. Though no one is certain how this will ultimately affect customer relationships, the odds are that it will catalyze even more switching between brands and products. Emerging leaders will need to determine how their new customer intimacy will evolve, how to communicate through technology in new ways, and how to forge a link that can withstand the impact of the Internet on customer relationships.

Getting into the Customer's Head and Heart

These nine themes are developed fully by Action Learning workshops. The workshops are not experts lecturing about the need to balance costs and long-term customer needs or about how customers cannot be managed. Instead, the themes emerge from direct experience with customers, through team discussions, and via feedback from coaches and top executives.

At G.E., cross-functional teams worked together on a number of customer issues. In the 1980s at G.E., it was a radical concept to have manufacturing, design, and financial people addressing customer issues. For instance, two cross-functional teams participated in an Action Learning project just prior to the removal of most trade barriers among European common market countries. The teams were asked to recommend a marketing strategy for G.E. Information Systems in Europe and to develop it from the customer's perspective.

To do so, the teams interviewed at least fifty current and prospective G.E. customers. For many team members, the intensive interviewing process was revelatory in and of itself. Many team members had never even talked to a customer before. When teams reconvened, participants bubbled over with ideas. For the first time, manufacturing managers were given the chance to offer their input about a customer issue; financial people had the opportunity to get their ideas heard. Certainly, many good recommendations emerged from these sessions. More importantly, broader customer issues surfaced. Sales people began to see how other functions might contribute to the solution of problems that they had previously considered no one's problems but their own. Other functional managers learned about the particularly vexing matters that salespeople faced when dealing with customers. Teams confronted those who clung to certain customer biases ("Driving sales costs down is our only priority" and "There is no such thing as brand loyalty, so why should we focus on anything but price and service?") and helped them recognize those biases for what they were. This cross-pollination of perspectives helped re-create leaders who became more holistic and visionary in their customer approach.

Action Learning also offers organizations the opportunity to work through the complexities that bedevil customer strategies. At Johnson & Johnson, Action Learning helped participants challenge their business proposition and perceive that a new customer was being born. The sales force in Johnson & Johnson's medical device and pharmaceutical companies knew the traditional customer well; they had developed historically strong relationships with doctors. But the buying power of an individual doctor is eroding and being replaced by a complex set of interdependencies. Hospital and HMO purchasing directors are now engaged in contract purchasing; new HMO organizations created by combining hospital chains and physician networks sometimes have little control over hospital purchasing departments. In addition, there were many different sales divisions for different products in the past—sterilizers, sutures, surgical supplies, etc. Now Johnson & Johnson has established one central contract representative, termed Health Care Systems, because customers are consolidating into one group (like an HMO). How does the company unify all its divisions and go to market with a single sales strategy?

Action Learning provides participants from different operating companies and functions the chance to test new ideas and unravel the intricate web of the health care market. The process gets them out talking to customers about what they really need and forces them to discuss whether Johnson & Johnson is equipped to provide it. Action Learning does not make all this simple, but it does allow intelligent managers to receive input about customers from multiple sources and sort through that information via a formalized process.

Perhaps the biggest benefit of Action Learning (relative to customer issues) is its ability to help participants make the transition from segregated to integrated mindsets. The marketplace used to be a simpler place. In a previous era, there were clear dividing lines between customers. Division A targeted one group of customers, and Division B targeted another group. In the complex world we now live in, however, the lines have blurred. It is not always clear what division within a company is matched with a certain type of customer, or whether a customer is not simultaneously a fierce competitor.

Unfortunately, internal politics and structures can keep the boundaries in place. In some companies, divisions compete against each other for the same customers. There is duplication of effort and confusion (in the customer's mind) about who to call for an overlapping service. One of Citibank's Action Learning programs was designed to help the best and brightest managers overcome these internal squabbles and consider what made sense for their mutual customer. It was not unusual for two divisions such as Global Relationship Bank and Emerging Markets to go after the same customer for loan business. Many corporate customers were puzzled (and put off) when three or more people from different Citibank groups would call on them in the same time frame, pitching the same business. Not only was this irritating to customers and prospects, but it was a waste of Citibank resources.

The Action Learning program gave participants a chance to see the absurdity of this internal competition. Action Learning forces dissimilar people from divergent backgrounds to work together. Though at first there may be tension between these people because of their different perspectives, they are under pressure to produce viable recommendations, so they must work through their differences. At Citibank, participants focused on the needs of their customers and used those needs to reshape how internal groups worked together.

Connecting with the Customer

One of the things organizations frequently remark upon is the process their people go through after intensive and extensive Action Learning customer interviews. We would be remiss if we did not share this process with you, because it really is what is most responsible for changing attitudes and behaviors toward customers. The process is how participants typically react to both their interviews with customers and their discussion and reflection about what they have learned. In most instances, the process breaks down into the following five reactions/revelations:

1. *Discovering what the customer is thinking, feeling, and needing.* For some, this is a new experience—they have never talked to a customer before. For others, it is a different experience— they have never talked to so many customers in such depth

before. In both cases, they have a rare opportunity to ask questions (related to their Action Learning project) and explore customer attitudes in a way they have never done before. Participants are uniformly energized by what they hear, and they come back to team meetings excited about sharing their discoveries.

2. *Recognizing that the customer has options*. This is a sobering realization. Participants learn first-hand that they do not have a lock on a customer and customers have more buying options than ever. The extraordinary and continuous effort required to keep a customer makes an impact. In every industry, it is still cheaper and more effective to keep a customer (when considering prospecting, developing, and closing costs) than to find a new one.

3. *Grasping the interdependencies between customer and company*. Many participants are surprised by how closely linked the customer's and the company's fates really are. They learn that it is no longer "us versus them"; that if one succeeds, so shall the other (and if one fails . . .).

4. *Personalizing the idea of the customer*. For many organizational leaders, customers are abstract concepts. Action Learning helps them hear the customer's voice and recognize that they are struggling over the same cost and cultural issues as they are within their own organizations. Just listening to the anecdotes customers tell helps participants empathize with customers.

5. *Walking in the customer's shoes*. When participants spend time at a customer's organization, listening to their concerns and seeing problems first hand, they often develop a bond with the customer. At Ohio Bell, an Action Learning executive returned from a customer site and spent the next day (on his own time) attempting to solve the service problems that he encountered. He suddenly felt compelled to do something about these problems; they had assumed a much greater

importance to him. The emotion in his customer contact's voice, the cumulative experience of spending hours with many customers, the one-on-one interactions—all of these things forced this manager to take action. We have even seen participants "switch sides." People who used to defend the organization against customer complaints sometimes take the side of customers in Action Learning team meetings, helping others in the group understand what the customer is really saying.

Actions and Learnings

Action Learning is designed to correct the common customer mistakes organizations make and to produce leaders who do not routinely make these mistakes. Consider whether your leaders demonstrate the following:

- Rarely talking to or visiting customers at their locations if they are not in marketing or sales.

- Treating customer problems and opportunities the same way they always have, despite a changing marketplace.

- Viewing the customer only through one's narrow functional perspective.

- Not listening to what the service people have to say about customers; thinking that service people are a "lower life-form" not worth listening to.

- Refusing to empower service people to solve customer problems or motivate them to want to do so.

- Hiring consultants to deal with customer problems (rather than attempting to investigate the problems on their own).

- Rationalizing difficulties with customers ("It's the economy" or "We can't offer the prices that our overseas competitors can") rather than examining them with a fresh eye.

- Believing price and service are the only things customers care about.

Establishing a customer-focused Action Learning program often depends on choosing challenging and meaningful business projects. The following is a list of different projects, some of which are challenging and meaningful, others of which are not. Place a check mark next to the ones that fit our criteria for Action Learning:

_____ Project 1: Hiring salespeople who are better "closers" than the ones you currently have.

_____ Project 2: Reducing cost-per-sale by 5 percent.

_____ Project 3: Finding a way to design new products that anticipate customer requirements.

_____ Project 4: Preparing the sales force for the social and economic trends that are affecting what a given market needs from its suppliers.

_____ Project 5: Exploring techniques to encourage networking and developing leads.

_____ Project 6: Determining whether the right people and policies are in place to capitalize on a rapidly growing South American market.

Correct Answers: 3, 4, 6.

Finally, here is an exercise that will test your willingness to launch an Action Learning program with a customer focus. See whether you (and/or management) can answer the following questions affirmatively:

1. Are you willing to have people who in the past have had little or no contact with customers spend many hours talking and visiting with them?

2. Are you willing to turn manufacturing, engineering, and operations people loose on customer issues, knowing that this might cause initial resentment among marketing and sales executives?

3. Are you prepared to implement recommendations of Action Learning teams that attempt to balance cost incentives with customer relationship incentives?

4. Are you prepared to implement recommendations of Action Learning teams that call for empowering customer service people to make decisions that circumvent traditional policies on behalf of customers?

5. Are you willing to re-create leaders who not only listen to customers but take the risk of anticipating customer needs and investing in products and services designed to meet those needs?

12

Reaching to the Future

Organizations are rapidly heading toward a leadership crisis and may be there already. People emerging from executive development programs or who have been groomed for leadership through succession planning are not up to the task. The way some companies adopt the latest leadership fad or bring in a guru to inspire executives to lead companies in new directions has almost a desperate quality.

We understand that desperation. For years companies have had the luxury of cloning people for top positions, replacing one command-and-control leader with another. We have experienced the frustration of the top teams unable to settle on clear criteria for leadership selection and development. Now it is extraordinarily difficult to make a list of new leadership requirements because that list keeps changing. One day you need a leader who can work across boundaries; the next you also need those who are skilled at managing diversity. Even more challenging is that the pace of change only keeps accelerating. As tough as it is to define what leadership is needed for your company today, it will be even tougher tomorrow.

On top of that, we are rapidly moving toward a time when the best leaders will be people who are comfortable working in highly complex, paradoxical, unstructured, and ambiguous environments. For instance, some common leadership requirements now include

- Working comfortably with a company that is both a collaborator and a competitor.

- Centralizing one part of an organization and decentralizing another part (that is, centralizing brand decisions and decentralizing local market product development).

- Creating and executing policies that are global in scope but that allow for local office innovation and initiative.

- Motivating a diverse workforce with vastly different values, ethnic backgrounds, languages, and work styles.

Preparing leaders through traditional executive development programs for these roles is very difficult. Preparing them by rotating them through "developmental" positions and hoping they pick up leadership traits on the job is equally difficult. Knowledge of leadership theory will hardly help anyone confront the chaos and complexity of the marketplace in the next century. It is hard to test new behaviors and develop new perspectives when you are enmeshed in the immediate demands of a career (no matter how developmental that job might be).

Action Learning provides leaders a chance to experiment with new behaviors. They may not learn everything they need to know, but they emerge from the program with one key attribute they may have lacked when they entered it. That attribute is increased self-awareness, and it will be something few twenty-first century leaders can do without.

Know Thyself, Know Thy Company

The margin for error is rapidly being reduced. Though in the past it might have been possible for leaders to function effectively despite blind spots, in coming years this liability will not be acceptable. We have known executives in the past who succeeded even though they were unaware of how their attitudes and behaviors affected those around them. In an environment of rapid change and daunting complexity, the unaware leader is a serious liability. People who work for and with him will not tolerate the negative behaviors that result; there will be too much performance pressure to allow for defensiveness or over-reaction. Consistent performance research demonstrates that the leader who can astutely assess the reactions of others is more likely to perform effectively.

Similarly, current leaders must recognize what their organizations are rather than what they were. At Shell, Tektronix, Ameritech, Johnson & Johnson, and many other companies, a great deal of wishful thinking and nostalgia dominated strategy. Executives can delude themselves into thinking that the company's current products are as competitive as before, or they fail to recognize that customer requirements have changed.

Action Learning can open participants' eyes—about themselves and their company. It is a process of self-discovery. It sends people out into the field to talk to customers rather than relying on reports and second-hand information. It provides feedback from numerous sources, reducing illusions and delusions. It offers time and techniques for reflection, giving participants the chance to absorb and integrate experiences. It is a crucible that puts pressure on each participant to analyze his or her attitudes and behaviors objectively and make changes if necessary.

Speed and flexibility will be two key traits of twenty-first century leaders. Leaders with self-awareness are more likely to move quickly, confidently, and in different directions without needing to be consistently "right" or in control. Self-awareness breeds confidence. Action Learning participants can become more confident in their abilities because they have gained insights about their strengths and weaknesses. When they encounter a tough assignment, they are less inhibited by the anxiety of "Will I be able to do that?" They are more clear about their own capabilities (as well as when they need to ask for help). They are not made overly anxious by new and unfamiliar situations, and consequently they are able to make faster decisions and take greater risks.

Twenty-First Century Scenarios

Although building self-awareness and learning to act on it will be underlying goals of all future executive development programs, these goals are not what will drive organizations to re-create their leaders. If our experience is any indication, most companies will ultimately utilize Action Learning because of specific business problems and opportunities—problems and opportunities that demand new leadership skills to address them effectively.

What will be the most pressing issues? What scenarios will recur and push organizations to re-create their leaders in order to deal with them? Here are some likely catalysts:

- *Moving from a domestic to a global mindset.* Most of our current clients are attempting to balance global and local approaches effectively. General Electric offers a paradigm for the problems many organizations will face in the twenty-first century and the possibilities for solving them through Action Learning. When G.E. embarked on Action Learning in the mid–1980s, their leadership was rooted in the United States. Recognizing the need to develop a cadre of global leaders and shift their business in an international direction, Action Learning workshops took people out of comfortable environments and had them pursue projects all over the world. Under challenging conditions, participants met foreign customers, learned about the culture of doing business in various parts of the world, and developed an appreciation for the obstacles and opportunities that existed. It is hard to think of any company that will not eventually need to transition its people from a domestic to a global perspective.

- *Responding to changing market realities.* As Peter Drucker has said, "Whom the gods wish to destroy, they send thirty years of success." Companies become locked into business theory and need re-created leaders to help them extricate themselves. We have seen many organizations trapped in one mode of doing business for years, unable or unwilling to recognize that their markets have shifted. We have conducted Action Learning programs for a consulting firm that thrived by focusing on local office productivity. Their leadership excelled at keeping costs down and fees up. What they did not excel at was synthesis—the ability to synthesize diverse ideas, think across boundaries, and create value in new ways. This is what their clients are now demanding, and it is a competence they need. All sorts of markets will be shifting, and Action Learning orients leaders to the shifts and adjust their thinking and behaviors accordingly.

- *Dealing with rapid growth.* We are seeing an increasing number of companies experiencing unprecedented growth. We are working with one firm that has a number of hot products, and these products are in great demand in many overseas markets. As a result, the company has signed up foreign distributors at a manic pace. Because they lack global managers, they have also hired people all over the world to supervise the introduction of these new products. Despite their hot products, they have suffered from high turnover, exorbitant recruitment costs, and difficulty integrating all the new hires into the culture. Action Learning can develop leaders with the confidence and fresh thinking necessary to deal with these rapid growth issues.

- *Working across boundaries*. Breaking down the barriers between functions, offices, business units, and other groups has already become an important goal of many companies, and it is going to be picked up by more of them as the benefits of a boundaryless organization gain wider recognition. Citibank's Team Challenge program has successfully addressed this issue, demonstrating that even silos that have been in place for years can be dismantled. Through its cross-functional teams, outdoor team-building activities, and a variety of other techniques, Action Learning smashes the biases and historical animosities that form the basis of boundaries.

- *Moving general managers into leadership positions*. Some companies routinely promote people from a given function into top positions. The Limited, for instance, has a history of naming merchants as store presidents, as they represent the company's core competency. Other organizations do not favor any particular function but generally choose people who excel in one specific area as their leaders. The problem, of course, is that there is a growing need for leaders who are really general managers and can think broadly, manage cross-functional teams, allocate resources fairly rather than functionally, and who can synthesize and integrate a cross-section of concepts and knowledge and come up with fresh ideas. Action Learning allows people with general management talent to shine. The process also helps people acquire and polish general management skills, because the projects people work on demand multi-dimensional thinking.

Breaking the Pattern

Organizations, like people, tend to fall into habits that are hard to break. Though the aforementioned issues certainly will drive companies to re-create their leaders, these companies may experience difficulty acting on this impulse. That is because bureaucracies tend to replicate themselves. One generation of leaders chooses the next generation in their own image. They choose people who went to the same schools, who share the same business philosophies, who "grew up" in the same functions, who belong to the same clubs. In an environment where management of diversity is critical, this is a pattern winning companies must break.

Action Learning helps them break it. Habitual behaviors and ingrained attitudes run deep, sometimes unconsciously, and Action Learning penetrates beyond the surface of most participants. People learn to appreciate the value of diversity in the Action Learning crucible, recognizing that they are dependent on people from different functions, backgrounds, and countries to do an effective job on the assigned project. Similarly, they learn to move away from the command-and-control style of leadership that some assumed was their corporate birthright.

It takes a process as intense and revealing as Action Learning to help people shift away from control-oriented behaviors: making all the decisions, wanting to know and control everything that is happening and closing deals. Despite all that has been written about how this leadership style is no longer viable, it is still an instinctive response for people in positions of responsibility, especially in times of crisis. Surprisingly, perhaps, it is a response common even for young executives. Working with a group of M.B.A.'s on a role-playing exercise recently, we assigned students roles such as president, vice presidents, directors, and so on. Almost uniformly, they responded to their roles by issuing orders and demanding performance. In debriefing, we asked them where they learned this style of leadership. They cited the heroic images of CEOs popularized by the media.

One future challenge organizations will face is helping their people become aware of their command-and-control tendencies and trade them in for more relevant leadership traits.

Identifying the New Leaders

Not everyone can manage their own tendencies to over-control. Not everyone can function effectively in a complex, ambiguous, fast-changing environment. Not everyone can be re-created.

Action Learning provides companies with a tool to identify twenty-first century leaders. More accurately, Action Learning lets twenty-first century leaders identify themselves. Every time we have run an Action Learning program, certain people have made contributions that demonstrated their potential for leadership. In many instances, these people would not have emerged—or emerged this quickly—in the course of everyday work life. Action Learning, however, gives participants the opportunity to be recognized. They may not be good politicians or they may lack the traditional images of leaders; often they have been unidentified and unrecognized for some time. Within Action Learning, however, the traditional procedures and policies are removed. People are unconstrained by what is "appropriate"; they are not buried under a structure of four reporting layers; they are encouraged to take risks and challenge assumptions.

At Ameritech, at one of the early vision workshops before the Action Learning program was initiated, the participants were asked to make recommendations about how the company might move forward. One of the groups had not arrived at a recommendation when they were asked to report to the CEO. Dennis, a member of the group, was a finance manager who was quite unassuming, even quiet. Yet within the Action Learning workshop, he demonstrated an unusual willingness to work with people across functions and keep an open mind. I (David) asked Dennis to make the report on the team's views. Dennis asked me what he should say, and I told him to speak from his heart, to talk honestly about the roadblocks, and express his feelings about what should be done to seize the important moment. This financial manager did just that, and management noticed. His conviction about what was going wrong and his commitment to finding a solution came through strongly. As a result of his report, Bill Weiss, the CEO of Ameritech, selected him for the lead team responsible for sponsoring Ameritech's Action Learning transformation.

Democratization: Taking the Process to the People

We have primarily focused on how Action Learning works as a formal process. Yet it can also work informally, and that is of significance for organizations in the future. Once companies have sponsored Action Learning workshops, they build a critical mass of change agents and re-created leaders. The process becomes sufficiently understood and widespread that it can be applied in ways less formal than those discussed here.

At Citibank, for instance, people are now using the Team Challenge model to deal with a wide range of issues. They have assembled teams across functions and business units and use Action Learning tools and techniques to generate fresh perspectives on problems. There is also a Team Challenge web site that describes various projects that are the focus of teams; employees are invited to visit the site, share their ideas and offer or receive advice. In addition, Team Challenge alumni are spreading the process through their leadership. Many of them routinely use the coaching and feedback tools to help others develop the attitudes and behaviors of recreated leaders. They also help others learn how to work across boundaries and facilitate change, just as they learned these things from Action Learning workshops.

Action Learning need not be an elitist process reserved only for leaders. That may be the presenting need, but it can eventually help a wide range of employees develop new competencies and address problematic issues. The democratization that has occurred at

Citibank will naturally occur at any organization that uses Action Learning in many different approaches.

Now and especially in the future, human resources will play a pivotal role in sponsoring Action Learning. In combination with line executives, human resources leaders are increasingly in the best position to initiate Action Learning. As their role within organizations evolves, they will be called upon to help create intellectual capital. They will be asked to challenge people, to push them to develop their capabilities, and to catalyze employees to think out of the box, become more creative, and contribute great new ideas. HR will assume a much more provocative role in the future. Perhaps it is heresy to suggest it, but they will purposefully raise employees' discomfort level, not with threats of termination but by challenging people—especially leaders—to reexamine their assumptions about the company. Intellectual capital is the competence that will be in great demand in the next century, and HR can encourage a process like Action Learning to amass that capital.

We do not want to oversell Action Learning as the solution for the leadership needs confronting companies throughout the world. Recruitment strategies, succession processes, and many other factors will affect how well a company deals with this crisis. Our point—and the point of this book—is that organizations need to inject reflection, feedback, cross-functional team experiences, "stretching" projects, and other Action Learning elements into the system. The new behaviors, attitudes, and ideas forged by these elements are an effective response to this crisis. Action Learning starts the ball rolling, producing the momentum necessary to recreate leaders who can transform organizations.

Resource A

Recommended Readings

Boude, D. and Associates (eds.). *Reflection: Turning Experience into Learning*. London: Kogan Page, 1985.

Chawla, S. and Renesch, J. (eds.). *Learning Organizations: Developing Cultures for Tomorrow's Workplace*. Portland: Productivity Press, 1993.

Inglis, S. *Making the Most of Action Learning*. Brookfield, VT: Gower Publishing, 1994.

Mai, R. P. *Learning Partnerships: How Leading American Companies Implement Organizational Learning*. Alexandria, VA: American Society for Training and Development.

Marquardt, M. J. Action learning. INFO-LINE, Apr. 1997, p. 16. Alexandria, VA: American Society for Training and Development.

Marquardt, M. J. *Building the Learning Organization: A Systems Approach to Quantum Improvement and Global Success*. New York: McGraw-Hill, 1996.

Marquardt, M. J. and Angus, R. *The Global Learning Organization: Gaining Competitive Advantage Through Continuous Learning*. Burr Ridge, IL: Irwin Professional Publishing, 1994.

Mumford, A. (ed.). *Action Learning at Work*. Brookfield, VT: Gower Publishing, 1997.

Mumford, A. (ed.). *Insights into Action Learning*. Bradford, England: MCB University Press, 1984.

Pedler, M. (ed.) *Action Learning in Practice, 3rd Edition*. Brookfield, VT: Gower Publishing, 1997.

Pedler, M. *Action Learning for Managers*. London: Lemos & Crane, 1996.

Pedler, M. (ed.), *Action Learning in Practice*. Aldershot, England: Gower Publishing, 1983, p. 297.

Senge, P. *The Fifth Discipline: The Art and Practice of the Learning Organization*.
New York: Doubleday, 1990.

Watkin, K. E. and Marsick, V. J. (eds.). *Creating the Learning Organization*.
Alexandria, VA: American Society for Training and Development, 1996.

Weinstein, K. *Action Learning: A Journey in Discovery and Development*. London:
HarperCollins, 1995.

Resource B

Action Learning Examples

Exhibit 1. Example of an Action Learning Process.

WORKSHOP 1
Building Blocks for Growth

Content:
1. NationsBank vision
2. Creating growth
3. Community activity
4. Building customer value
5. Technology
6. Driving value
7. CEO guest speaker
8. Building a market-focused organization
9. 360-assessment feedback

Team Projects
1. Establish teams
2. Clarify charters
3. Develop project plans

Work on Projects

Tasks:
1. Conduct benchmark visits
2. Gather and analyze information
3. Develop preliminary positions for Workshop 2

Processes:
1. Team development
2. Multi-tasking

WORKSHOP 2
Check-In

Content:
1. The future of financial services
2. Financial analysts' views of NationsBank
3. Competitive analysis of the financial services industry

Preliminary Reports
1. Context
   • Major trends, issues, considerations, and so on relating to the topic
2. Focus
   • Status report on how NationsBank can benefit the most, given the context
3. Major issues and challenges
4. Next steps

Team Feedback

Work on Projects

Tasks:
1. Conduct benchmark visits
2. Gather and analyze information
3. Generate final reports or recommendations

Processes:
1. Conflict management
2. Feedback
3. Key decision making

WORKSHOP 3
Achieving the Vision

Content:
1. Commitments to act
2. Feedback on reports

Final Reports

Specific recommendations and supporting rationale for assigned project

Exhibit 2. Example of Workshop 1 Agenda.

	Day 1: **Creating Growth** Facilitator: ___	Day 2: **Building Customer Value** Facilitator: ___	Day 3: **Driving Value** Facilitator: ___	Day 4: **Building a Market-Focused Organization** Facilitator: ___
8:00	1. Welcome	12. Introduce building customer value	20. Introduce driving value	27. Introduce building a market-focused organization
8:15	2. Prework debrief	13. Building customer value	21. Driving value	28. Building a market-focused organization
8:45	3. Opening remarks			
9:15	4. Introduce creating growth			
9:30	5. Creating growth			
12:15	6. Morning wrap-up			
12:30	7. Prep for community activity			
12:45		14. Morning wrap-up Lunch	22. Morning wrap-up	29. Morning wrap-up
1:00	*Lunch* (and travel to activity)	*Lunch*	*Lunch*	*Lunch*
2:00	8. Community activity	15. 360-degree feedback	23. Fishbowl discussion	30. Action planning
3:00		16. Teams begin work on assignments		
3:30			24. Group team building	31. Wrap-up
4:00				*Adjourn*
5:00	9. Subteam debrief of community activity	17. Prepare for "fishbowl" discussion		
6:00	*Dinner*	*Dinner*	*Dinner*	
7:30	10. Large group debrief of community activity	18. Introduce technology speaker	25. Introduce guest speaker	
8:15	11. Project team assignments and team process overview	19. Guest speaker: technology guru	26. Guest speaker: CEO of growth company	

Exhibit 3. Example of Leading Growth Team Questions.

I. How Do We Make NationsBank the Dominant Brand in the Financial Services Industry?

In a marketplace characterized by information and advertising overload, what must NationsBank do to become the premier, recognized, and most respected brand in the financial services industry? What must we do to make current and potential consumer and commercial customers think of NationsBank first when they are asked to name the premier service and financial institution? What should NationsBank as a brand symbolize—and what must we do in order to create that positioning and stature in the marketplace?

As a team, you are chartered to do four things:

First, identify world-class companies and their brands and determine how world-class companies achieve brand preeminence. What can we learn from them, and what should we apply to NationsBank in order to become the best?

Second, complete a comprehensive analysis of our current brand position in the marketplace, using existing resources, available research we have done or chartered others to do for us, and investigate additional important questions which have not been asked. Implicit in every brand is a statement of values and culture—what does ours represent, and what should it? As a team, identify the important issues which we must address to create a predominant brand, including internal and external obstacles, cost, strategic direction, leadership, and traditions.

Third, the team should build an action plan which addresses at least the following:

1. How will NationsBank become the widely known and respected branch in both the financial and service industries?

Exhibit 3. Example of Leading Growth Team Questions *(continued)*.

2. What do we want the NationsBank brand to represent in the future?

3. What will it cost to achieve this goal, and what are the relative costs and benefits of achieving it—given the aspirations of the other teams?

4. What new products and services must be developed in order to create a predominant brand in the marketplace?

5. How will we balance the requirements of a strong brand with the importance of recognizable products?

6. How do we make brand meaningful to our associates?

7. How must we coordinate and develop our internal resources and people in order to aggressively create a dominant brand?

8. Are we leveraging the potential and power of our brand, and what must we do in order to aggressively create a dominant brand?

9. What must be done to ensure that NationsBank is the symbol of quality and integrity? How do we manage our risks in order to achieve maximum growth while preserving the integrity of our brand? How do we measure success?

10. What are the tradeoffs between the investment required to establish the supremacy of the NationsBank brand and the potential returns?

11. What degree of consistency is required across the products of NationsBank in order to establish a clear brand position?

12. How do we best leverage technology in becoming the dominant brand?

Finally, as a team, identify the potential risks in our efforts to establish the preeminent brand and what should be done to manage that risk. In becoming the premier brand in financial services, what is our Achilles' heel, and what must be done about it?

Exhibit 3. Example of Leading Growth Team Questions *(continued).*

II. How Can We Grow and Develop the Leadership Talent and Depth Required to Fuel Growth?

Given that a strong committed cadre of leaders who execute a strategy is the only resource not available for sale or purchase to a corporation today—what must NationsBank do over the next five years to increase the supply and capability of our leadership? This group should look at future projections for leadership needs in the bank and determine if the current methods for growing leadership talent will meet those needs.

As a team you are chartered to do five things:

First, identify those companies within and outside the financial services industry that are world class in the identification, development, promotion, and reward of leaders. What do these companies do, and how do they differ from NationsBank? What is the link between their leadership development system and their business and financial performance? What are the most important lessons from these world-class companies for NationsBank?

Second, this team should describe the current system for leadership development in NationsBank and decide if our current approach is world class. In particular, examine how this team will determine whether there is a sufficient diversity of thinking, ideas, experience, perspective, background, and demographics in our leadership ranks, as well as ability to manage diversity.

Third, Examine how we promote the type of openness, challenge, and trust among our leaders which would be indicative of our strength and self-confidence. Are the skills and attributes of our current leadership pool sufficient to meet the challenge of our future business? If there is a gap, what must be done to close it?

Exhibit 3. Example of Leading Growth Team Questions (continued).

Fourth, examine what systems need to be implemented to assure us of a continuous supply of capable leaders who will make sure we win. How do we recruit the best, identify the best among us, reward them, and develop them? What critical experiences should tomorrow's leaders be having today, and how can we ensure they are obtaining them?

This team should identify and recommend the most important actions which NationsBank must take to become world class in the development of executive leadership talent.

The team should address these specific issues:

1. Do we have an adequate supply of leadership talent to meet our growth projections?
2. Does our current executive leadership have the needed skills to grow our business?
3. Do we have sufficient diversity and differences among our leadership to stimulate our growth?
4. What must we do to create a learning environment that encourages growth through shared knowledge and experiences?
5. What should we be doing to find, identify, promote, develop, and reward leadership?
6. What should be our standards of leadership for future success, and how do we measure our leaders against those standards?
7. How should we honestly appraise and communicate that appraisal to executives? What should be the criteria for evaluation of key leaders?
8. What must we do in order to retain key leadership talent—both internal and external hires?
9. How do we leverage technology to share current knowledge within the organization as well as new learnings and information?

Exhibit 3. Example of Leading Growth Team Questions (*continued*).

Finally, this team should identify our Achilles' heel in leadership development. What are the most significant obstacles now and in the future, and how can we overcome them?

Index

A

Aberthal, L., 119

Action Learning: advantages of, 69–81; attention grabbers for, 152–154; business projects for, 90, 153–154, 183; catalysts for, 6, 13, 49–50, 57–60, 61–63, 152–154; Change Checklist for, 160; companies that have used, 1–2; contraindications for, 7–8; for cross-functionality, 99–113; cumulative impact of, 130; customer-focused, 171–184; democratization of, 193–194; early experiences with, 2–5; elements of, 14–15, 16–33; experiences of, stories of, 35–37; factors in success of, 63–65, 78–80; framework of, 13–34; freedom to act in, 140–142; for future change, 185–194; gestalt of, 15–16, 78; for global leadership, 83–97; graduates of, 142–145; historical development of, 1–2; holistic approach of, 10, 69, 76–78; for independent thinking and action, 135–148; for individual change, 149–160; methodologies of, 121–124; versus other leadership development methods, 69–73, 76–78; planning global, 87–89; problems caused by, 143–145; for

reconceptualizing the business, 115–134; re-created leaders and, 49–66; regular use of, 130; safe environment of, 124, 134, 140–142; for technology-business integration, 161–170; temporary system of, 15–16, 46–47, 78, 122, 132–133, 149–150; versatility of, 5–7, 46–47. See also Global Action Learning; Leaders, re-created; Leadership re-creation; Twelve-element framework

Action Learning graduates: positive impact of, 142–143; tensions caused by, 143–145

Action Learning team formation, 24–25. See also Participant selection

Actions and Learnings, 9; for change, 159–160; for cross-functionality, 111–113; for customer relationships, 182–184; for global leadership, 96–97; for independent thinking and action, 146–148; for leadership re-creation, 80–81; for reconceptualization, 131–134; for technology-business integration, 168–170

Ambiguous business environment. See Business environment

Ameritech, 1, 13–14, 61, 139, 187; Breakthrough Leadership team of,

Ameritech *(continued)*
110–111; catalyst for change of, 6, 61–62, 138, 152–153; cross-functional Action Learning of, 104, 109–111; customer focus of, 171, 175; reconceptualization Action Learning of, 120–121, 133, 192–193; re-created leadership of, 51; sponsorship in, 60; strategic mandate of, 19; technology-business integration of, 162, 169; transformation of, 77

Arthur Anderson, 1, 6–7, 24; coaching global partners at, 46; Global Action Learning story of, 93

Artificial intelligence, 164–165

AT&T, 59

Automation, moving beyond, 165–166

B

Balanced Business Scorecard, 39

Behavior-based programs, 73, 80

Beliefs: confrontation of, 123, 133, 139–140; self-awareness of, 138–140

BellSouth, 1, 137

Benchmarking, 61, 170

Best-practices study method, 71–72, 80

Big-picture thinking, for technology, 166

Boundaryless organizations, 49; Action Learning for, 99–113; flexibility and, 74–75; in twenty-first century, 190. *See also* Cross-functionality; Functional model

Breakthrough mentality, 75

Bureaucratic mindset, 135

Business environment, complex/global/ambiguous/paradoxical, 49; future of, 185–194; leadership skills needed for, 73–76, 185–186; re-created leaders for, 50–60, 185–194. *See also* Global Action Learning; Global leadership

Business projects, in Action Learning, 90, 153–154, 183

Business proposition, 174

Business school model, 71–72, 80

Business strategy: leadership re-creation linkage to, 80; technology integrated with, 161–170

C

Career stage openness, 79

Carroll, P., 24, 43, 51

Case study method, 71–72, 80

Catalysts: in Action Learning process, 138–140, 152–154; reconceptualizing, 121–124; for re-creation, 49–51, 57–60, 61–63; of twenty-first century, 188–190; for undertaking Action Learning, 6, 13, 61–63, 188–190; for undertaking Global Action Learning, 90, 190–191. *See also* Strategic mandate; Stretch issues

Censorship, of traditional leadership, 56–57

Center for Creative Leadership, 73

Change: catalysts for, 49–50, 61–63; evaluating approaches to, 159–160; factors in success of, 63–65; future, 185–194; General Electric story of, 154–158; hubris and, 65–66; of individuals, 149–160; need for fast, 149, 185–194; need for re-creation and, 57–60, 185–194; organizational, and individual ability to, 149–150; organizational errors of, 159; questions for evaluating, 159–160; resistance to, 117, 150–151. *See also* Individual change; Reconceptualization

Change Acceleration Process (CAP), 156–158

Change Checklist for Action Learning, 160

Change management, failure of, 151–152. *See also* Individual change

Change management methods, traditional, prevalence of, 8. *See also* Executive development programs; Leadership re-creation

"Change question," for participant selection, 23

Charan, R., 1, 5

Chief executive officers (CEOs): securing the support of, 17–18, 61; as visionary heroes, 116–119, 191. *See also* Leaders, re-created; Sponsor

Citibank, 1; Action Learning stories of, 35–42, 141; Balanced Business Scorecard, 39; catalyst for change of, 63; cross-functional Action Learning story of, 36–38, 106–108, 190; cultural change at, 35–38; customer focus of, 171, 179–180; human resource development at, 38–42; learning process roadmap of, 21, 22; participant recognition at, 24; presentations at, 31; sponsorship in, 17, 36; strategic mandate of, 19; Team Challenge program, 5, 21, 22, 35–38, 107–108, 141, 163–164, 190, 193–194; technology-business integration of, 163–164

Closure, 33

Coaching, 26–27; in Citibank stories, 38, 42; equal-opportunity, 81; limitations of, 70

Cognitive learning, 80

Command-and-control leadership, 51–57, 191–192

Commitment: to Action Learning, 64; to cross-functionality, 103; to re-creation of leaders, 60–61. *See also* Sponsor

Competitive advantage, 53; leadership skills needed for, 73–76; openness to sources of, 59; of re-created leaders, 57–60

Complex business environment. *See* Business environment

Confrontation, of beliefs and behaviors, 123, 133, 138–140

Cost-benefit mentality, for technology, 166

Crisis, as catalyst, 61–63

Cross-cultural differences, 88–89, 94–95. *See also* Global Action Learning; Global leadership

Cross-functionality: Action Learning for, 99–113; Actions and Learnings for, 111–113; Ameritech Action Learning program for, 109–111; Citibank Action Learning program for, 36–38, 106–108; cross-functional teams composition and, 103; customer relationships and, 177–178, 179–180; elements of Action Learning programs for, 112–113; empowerment and, 102–103; failure of, causes of, 102–103; functional prejudices and, 101–102, 105, 109–111, 112–113; outsider interaction and, 103–104; participation in high-level strategy-making and, 104–105; re-created leaders for, 54; resistance to, causes of, 100–102; team exercises for, 105, 112–113; in twenty-first century, 190. *See also* Boundaryless organizations; Functional model

Cross-functional team composition, 103

Crotonville Management Development Institute, 4–5, 126–127, 154

Cultural bias, 88–89

Cultural change: Citibank story of, 35–38; indications for success of, 63–65; openness to, 64. *See also* Change

Customer relationships: Action Learning for, 171–184; Action Learning business projects for, 183; boundary breaking for, 179–180; centralized cost decisions and, 175–176; challenging the business proposition and, 174; common mistakes in, 182–183; versus controlling of customers, 173–174;

Customer relationships (*continued*)
cross-functionality and, 177–178,
179–180; customer service representative empowerment and,
176–177; direct contact and, 171,
177, 180–182; 80/20 rule and,
176–177; evaluating current
approach to, 182–183; evaluating
readiness to change, 183–184;
Internet and, 173, 177; methods of
working on, 177; nine themes of,
172–177; salespeople's incentives
for, 175–176; stories of, 177–180

Customer service representatives,
empowerment/disempowerment of,
176–177

Customers: anticipating future needs
of, 174–175; companies' distrust of,
176; direct contact with, 171, 177,
180–182; goals of, 174; internal
competition for, 179–180; new requirements and resources of,
172–173

D

Data analysis, 28–29
Data gathering, 28; in Citibank story,
37–38; for reconceptualization,
121–122, 128–129, 132
Debriefing. *See* Reflection
Democratization, 193–194
Developmental assignments, 73
Dirty Dozen, The, 110–111
Doomsday scenarios, exposure to, 131
Draft presentation, 30; in Citibank
story, 38
Drucker, P., 28, 189
Dunlop, A., 116

E

Education, in Action Learning
process, 27
Electronic Data Systems (EDS),
119–121
80/20 customer rule, 176–177
Emotional energy, of re-created leaders, 55

Emotional engagement, in leadership
re-creation, 79
Emotional learning, 72, 80, 132; for
individual change, 151–153; for
self-knowledge, 138–140
Employee relationship, new, 75
Endosurgery, 120
Executive development programs, traditional: failure of, 13–14, 57; formal methods of, 71–73; informal
methods and, 70–71; prevalence of,
8; shortcomings of, 70–77, 186;
skills neglected in, 73–76
Executive education/business school
model, 71–72, 80
Exercises. *See* Actions and Learnings;
Outdoor activities; Team exercises
Extranet, 173

F

Fads, 64
Faith, of re-created leaders, 55–56
Feedback: in Citibank story, 42; and
coaching, 26–27, 42; in Global
Action Learning, 89–90; in leadership re-creation, 81; for reconceptualization, 123, 133; re-created
leaders' openness to, 56–57; for
self-awareness, 138–140; in Shell
Oil story, 45–46; for trust building,
89–90. *See also* 360-degree feedback
Final presentation, 30–31; in
Citibank story, 38; in General Electric story, 129–130
Flexibility: of Action Learning framework, 33–34, 46–47; for rapid
change, 187–188; of re-created
leaders, 59–60, 74–76, 187–188
Formal leadership training, 71–73
Fortune, 54
Free speech, and re-created leaders,
56–57
Fresco, P., 84, 125, 129
Fresh thinking: Action Research for,
135–148; and reconceptualization,
118, 132–133. *See also* Independent
thinking and action

Fun activities, 33
Functional model, 49, 81; assessment of, in one's organization, 111–112; history of, 99–102; reasons for persistence of, 100–102; traditional leaders and, 54. See also Boundaryless organizations; Cross-functionality
Functions: antipathy between, 101–102, 105, 109–111, 112–113; working outside of one's, 104. See also Cross-functionality

G

Gainey Farm, 3–4
Gates, B., 116
General Electric (G.E.), 13–14, 58, 130; Action Learning development at, 1, 4–5; Action Learning stories of, 154–158; Action Learning team of, 25; Change Acceleration Process (CAP) of, 156–158; change initiatives of, 154–158; cross-functional Action Learning of, 104; customer focus of, 171, 177–178; data gathering of, 121–122; Global Action Learning stories of, 84–87, 125–130, 188–189; Heidelberg executive development course of, 85–86; leadership competencies of, 136, 137, 158; Leadership Effectiveness Survey (LES) of, 85–86; manager's journal entries from, 125–130; Model for Change, 157; reconceptualization story of, 125–130; re-created leadership of, 51, 54; reflection session of, 32–33; sponsorship in, 17, 60–61; strategic mandate of, 19; technology-business integration of, 164–165; Work Out sessions of, 154–156
General Electric Capital, 164–165
General Electric Information Systems, 104, 178
General Electric International, 125
General Electric Power Systems, 156
General managers, 190

Generalists, 54
Glen Cove, 37
Global Action Learning programs, 83–97; Actions and Learnings for, 96–97; Arthur Andersen story of, 93; catalysts for, 90; common elements of, 90; customer focus in, 177–178; do's and don'ts for, 96–97; General Electric story of, 84–87, 125–130; Johnson & Johnson story of, 91–92; on-site location of, 90; participant selection for, 90; planning, 87–89; rationale for, 93–95; steering group for, 90; trust building in, 89–90; variations of, 90–93
Global business marketplace, 49; in twenty-first century, 188–189. See also Business environment
Global leadership, 49; Action Learning for, 83–97, 188–189; cross-cultural differences and, 88–89, 94–95; General Electric story of, 84–87; issues of, 88–89; key skill for, 83–84; as mindset versus location, 87; need for re-creation and, 58, 93–95; obstacles to, 84–85, 94–95, 150; trust building and, 89–90; for twenty-first century, 188–189; vertical and horizontal, 88. See also Leaders, re-created
Growth, rapid, 60, 189–190
Gurus, 71

H

Habitual behavior, breaking the pattern of, 191–192
Hagberg, R., 54
Health Care Systems, 179
Holistic approach, 10, 69, 76–78
Honeywell: Action Learning development at, 1, 2–4; dilemma of, 6
Hubris, 65–66
Human resources (HR) departments: commitment of, 64–65; sponsoring by, 194
Human resources development, Citibank story of, 38–42

I

IBM, 59, 65

Independent thinking and action: Action Learning for, 135–148; Action Learning environment for, 140–142; Actions and Learnings for, 146–148; defining leadership competencies for, 136–137, 146–147; developing an Action Learning program for, 146–148; impact of, on organization, 142–145; mixed messages about, 135; organizational environment and, 145–146; problems of, 143–145; questions for provoking, 147; rewarding and recognition of, 146, 148; self-awareness and, 138–140. *See also* Fresh thinking

Individual change: Action Learning for, 149–160; Actions and Learnings for, 159–160; attention grabbers for, 152–154; change management programs and, 151–152; General Electric story of, 154–158; organizational change and, 149–150; real work projects and, 153; resistance to, 150–151; theory of the case and, 153–154. *See also* Change

Informal leadership training, 70–71

Information: of customers, 172–173; and data gathering, 28; and orientation to issue, 27. *See also* Data gathering

Information sharing, thought-provoking, 121–122, 131–132

Intel, 118

Internet, 163–164; customers and, 173, 177

Interviews: customer, 172, 180–182; for reconceptualization data gathering, 121–122, 128–129, 132

Intranet, 173

Involvement versus isolation of leaders, 54

Issues. *See* Catalysts; Orientation to issue; Stretch issues

J

Johnson & Johnson, 1, 6, 53, 61, 130, 140, 143–144, 187; cross-functional Action Learning of, 104; customer focus of, 171, 178–179; data gathering of, 121–122; Global Action Learning story of, 91–92; leadership competencies of, 136; reconceptualization of, 120, 121–122; strategic mandate of, 19; technology-business integration of, 162

K

Kodak, 59

L

Lateral assignments, 54, 73

Laurent, A., 94–95

Leaders, re-created, 1; for future change, 185–194; general managers as potential, 190; identifying potential, 192–193; need for, 49–51, 57–60; qualities of, 51–57, 185–186; self-awareness of, 75–76, 138–140, 186–188; skills needed of, 73–76, 185–186; technology and, 58, 167–168; traditional leaders versus, 51–57. *See also* Action Learning; Global Action Learning; Global leadership

Leadership competencies, 51–52; defining, 136–137, 146–147; for future business environment, 185–186; for re-created leaders, 73–76

Leadership development. *See* Executive development programs; Leadership re-creation

Leadership Effectiveness Survey (LES), 85–86

Leadership models, defining of, 136–137, 146–147

Leadership re-creation: Actions and Learnings for, 80–81; for cross-functional leadership, 108–111, 112–113; factors in successful, 78–80; formal methods of, 71–73;

for future change, 185–194; general
managers as candidates for, 190;
identifying candidates for, 192–193;
increasing the odds of, 78–80; independent thinking and action in,
135–148; indications for success of,
63–65; informal methods of, 70–71;
methods of, 69–81; need for commitment to, 60–61; obstacles to,
191–192; for reconceptualizing the
business, 115–116; versus recruitment, 49–50; reinforcement of,
79–81; secrets of success of, 76–
78; technology and, 166–167. See
also Action Learning; Cross-
functionality; Global Action
Learning; Global leadership; Independent thinking and action;
Reconceptualization
Lean mentality, 101
Learn/stretch capacity, 75
Learning team formation, 24–25; in
Citibank story, 37
"Let 1000 flowers bloom" philosophy,
36, 38
Levi Strauss & Co., 2
Location: for Global Action Learning workshops, 90; for reconceptualization Action Learning sessions,
132

M
Market change, 189. See also Business
environment
Menezes, V., 17, 24, 36
Mentors, 70
Microsoft, 53, 59, 118
Military organization, 99–100
Mindsets, 135. See also Independent
thinking and action
Murphy's Law, 55

N
NationsBank, 1; Action Learning
process of, 198–204; catalyst for
change of, 6, 138; customer focus
of, 171; Leading Growth Team

questions of, 199–204; technology-
business integration of, 162
Nike, 118
Nortel (Northern Telecom), 1
Notebaert, D., 62, 175

O
Ohio Bell, 181–182
Older managers, and technology, 166
On-the-job training, 70
Organization size, and functional per-
sistence, 101
Organizational socialization, and
functional persistence, 100–101
Orientation to issue, 27; in Citibank
story, 37–38; in Shell Oil story,
43–44
Outdoor activities: in Action Learn-
ing experience, 37; for Global
Action Learning, 90; for leadership
development, 72; for "rapid team
building," 91–92; for reconceptual-
ization, 132; for self-awareness, 138;
for trust building, 90
Outward Bound, 72
Owners versus managers, 53

P
Paradoxical business environment.
See Business environment
Parallel world, for reconceptualiza-
tion, 122, 132–133. See also Tempo-
rary system
Participant selection, 21, 23–24; in
Citibank story, 37; democratization
and, 193–194; for Global Action
Learning, 90; for technology
Action Learning projects, 170;
tools for, 23. See also Learning team
formation
Performance improvement, Shell Oil
story of, 42–46
Performance pressure, 29, 127–128
Perot, R., 119
Phillips, L., 38–39
Physical exercises. See Outdoor
activities

Planful opportunism, 59
Political mapping tool, 30
Post-it notes, for participant selection, 23
Prejudices. See Cultural bias; Functions: antipathy between
Presentation. See Draft presentation; Final presentation
Process redesign, moving beyond, 165–166
Provocative information, 121–122, 131–132
Prussian army, 99–100
Psychological edge, in reconceptualization, 117–118

R

Rapid growth, 60, 189–190
"Rapid team building" exercise, 91–92
Re-creation of leaders. See Action Learning; Leaders, re-created; Leadership re-creation
Receptivity, of re-created leaders, 56, 59
Recognition, of independent thinkers, 146, 148
Reconceptualization: Action Learning for, 115–134; Actions and Learnings for, 131–134; confrontation of beliefs and behaviors for, 123, 133; cumulative impact of, 130; data gathering for, 121–122, 128–129; General Electric story of, 125–130; by leaders at all levels, 116–119; methodologies of, 121–124, 131–134; open and safe environment for, 124, 134; provocative data sharing for, 121–122, 131–132; self-reflection for, 123; stories of, 119–121; temporary system for, 122, 132–133; theory of the case for, 123–124, 133–134
Reed, J., 31, 37, 38, 63, 141, 163
Reflection, 31–33; critical importance of, 47; in leadership re-creation, 81; for reconceptualization, 123; of re-

created leaders, 55; in Shell Oil story, 46; on technology, 168; tools for, 32. See also Self-awareness
Reframing the business. See Reconceptualization
Rejecting behavior, of traditional leaders, 56
Resistance: Action Learning impact and, 144–145; to change, 117; to cross-functionality, 100–102; in individual change, 150–151
Reward systems, and independent thinking/action, 146, 148
Risk taking, in leadership re-creation, 81
Roadmaps, learning process, 20–21; example of, 22
Rotation, 54, 73, 186
Royal Dutch, 42–46

S

Salespeople, incentives for, 175–176
Scott paper, 116
Sears, 59
Selden, L., 43–44
Selection. See Participant selection
Self-awareness: for independent thinking and action, 138–140; and rapid change, 186–188; of re-created leaders, 75–76, 138–140, 186–188
Shell Oil, 1, 13–14, 33, 61, 187; Action Learning goals of, 7; Action Learning stories of 42–46, 139, 142; Action Learning team of, 24–25; change at, 152; cross-functional Action Learning of, 104, 141–142; participant recognition at, 24; performance improvement at, 42–46; reconceptualization of, 124; re-created leadership of, 51; strategic mandate of, 19; technology-business integration of, 162
Skepticism, of traditional leaders, 55
Sponsor(s), 16–19, 60–61; in Citibank stories, 36, 38–39; human

resources as, 194; for technology Action Learning project, 169; tools for enlisting, 17–18, 61

Steering group, for Global Action Learning, 90

Strategic mandate, 19–20; in Citibank story, 36. *See also* Change: catalysts for; Stretch issues

Strategy-making, participation in, 104–105. *See also* Reconceptualization

Stress, of Action Learning programs: for building cross-functionality, 104; temporary system and, 106. *See also* Tension level

Stretch issues, 19–20, 29; leadership skills for, 75. *See also* Strategic mandate

Succession planning, 81

Sunbeam, 116

T

Team exercises: for cross-functional Action Learning, 105, 112–113; for reconceptualization, 132. *See also* Actions and Learnings; Outdoor activities

Technocrats, 167

Technology: Action Learning for, 161–170; Action Learning stories of, 162–165; Action Learning tools for, 170; Actions and Learnings for, 168–10; developing an Action Learning program for, 169–170; evaluating problems of, 168–169; integration of, with business, 161–170; issues of, 165–168; issues of, analyzing, 169–170; and need for re-recreation, 58; and reconceptualizers at all levels, 117

Technophobes, 167

Tektronix, 138, 187

Temporary system, 15–16, 46–47, 78; for fast change, 149–150; for reconceptualization, 122, 132–133

Tension level: fun activities for breaking, 33; temporary system and, 78. *See also* Stress

The Limited, 190

Theory of the case, 41; and individual change, 153–154; and reconceptualization, 123–124, 133–134

360-degree feedback: in Citibank story, 42; and coaching, 26–27, 42; in cross-functional Action Learning, 109–110; in General Electric story, 126–127; in Global Action Learning, 89–90; manager's experience of, 126–127; method of, 73; in Shell Oil story, 45–46; for technology Action Learning projects, 170; for trust building, 89–90. *See also* Feedback

Tichy, N., 1, 3, 5

Time-based competition, 74

Trust building, in Global Action Learning, 89–90

Turboville, P., 43

Twelve-element framework of Action Learning, 14–15; coaching element of, 26–27; data analysis element of, 28–29; data-gathering element of, 28; draft presentation element of, 30; implementation of, stories of, 35–47; learning-process roadmap of, 20–21; learning team formation in, 24–25; orientation-to-issue element of, 27; participant selection element of, 21, 23–24; presentation element of, 30–31; reflection element of, 31–33; sponsor element of, 16–19; strategic mandate element of, 19–20; variations on, 33–34

Twenty-first century scenarios, 188–190

U

University of Michigan, 121–122

V

Van Orden, P., 17

Vertical-horizontal integration, 88

Visionary thinking, environment for, 124, 134
Visioning. *See* Reconceptualization

W
Walton, S., 116
Weiss, B., 51, 60, 61–62, 193

Welch, J., 4, 5, 17, 31, 15, 54, 60–61, 84, 87, 116, 125, 127, 130, 154, 157
"What if" scenarios, 124, 134
Whitman, W., 51
"Win as Much as You Can" exercise, 105
Work Outs, 154–158